Dynamic Language Embedding
With Homogeneous Tool Support

Inauguraldissertation
der Philosophisch-naturwissenschaftlichen Fakultät
der Universität Bern

vorgelegt von
Lukas Renggli
von Entlebuch

Leiter der Arbeit:
Prof. Dr. O. Nierstrasz

Institut für Informatik und angewandte Mathematik

Acknowledgements

First of all, I would like to express my gratitude to Oscar Nierstrasz for giving me the opportunity to work at the Software Composition Group. I thank him for his advice and support throughout the years.

I would like to thank Ralf Lämmel for writing the Koreferat and for accepting to be on the PhD committee. I enjoyed the good discussions we had when we met in Bern, Koblenz and at various language engineering conferences.

I thank Matthias Zwicker for accepting to chair the examination.

I am grateful to Stéphane Ducasse for his enthusiasm and the numerous invitations to join him at his research group in Annecy and later in Lille. I might not have taken the path of pursuing a PhD without the encouragements of him.

I also thank Tudor Gîrba for the inspiring discussions and for providing many of the ideas that have influenced this work.

I am much obliged to the people that provided constructive feedback on early drafts of this dissertation: Jorge Ressia, Fabrizio Perin, and Tudor Gîrba. I also thank my father Martin Renggli for the original cover art.

I would like to thank my master student Philipp Bunge, and my bachelor students Andrea Quadri and Max Leske for the hours we shared discussing and implementing new and exciting Smalltalk projects.

I am thankful to the Hilfsassistants of the lecture *Introduction to Software Engineering* that helped running the exercise hours in the past four years: Camillo Bruni, Philipp Bunge, Christian Bürgi, Stefan Ott, Patrik Rauber, Stefan Reichhart, Erwann Wernli, and Rafael Wampfler.

I would like to thank all the former and current members of the *Software Composition Group*. It was a pleasure to work with you: Gabriela Arévalo, Alexandre Bergel, Marcus Denker, Markus Gaelli, Orla Greevy, Adrian Kuhn, Adrian Lienhard, Mircea Lungu, Fabrizio Perin, Laura Ponisio, Jorge Ressia, David Röthlisberger, Niko Schwarz, Toon Verwaest, and Erwann Wernli. Special thanks go to Therese Schmid and Iris Keller that made the administrative work a pleasure.

I am grateful to my parents who have supported me all those years. I would like to express my thanks to my friends: Adriaan van Os for being ready to discuss anything despite the distance; and Jorge Ressia and Fabrizio Perin for the tools we implemented and the Argentine Empanadas, Italian Pizzoccheri, and Bernese Rösti we enjoyed.

Lukas Renggli
October 20, 2010

Abstract

Domain-specific languages (DSLs) are increasingly used as embedded languages within general-purpose host languages. DSLs provide a compact, dedicated syntax for specifying parts of an application related to specialized domains. Unfortunately, such language extensions typically do not integrate well with existing development tools. Editors, compilers and debuggers are either unaware of the extensions, or must be adapted at a non-trivial cost. Furthermore, these embedded languages typically conflict with the grammar of the host language and make it difficult to write hybrid code; few mechanisms exist to control the scope and usage of multiple tightly interconnected embedded languages.

In this dissertation we present *Helvetia*, a novel approach to embed languages into an existing host language by leveraging the underlying representation of the host language used by these tools. We introduce *Language Boxes*, an approach that offers a simple, modular mechanism to encapsulate (i) compositional changes to the host language, (ii) transformations to address various concerns such as compilation and syntax highlighting, and (iii) scoping rules to control visibility of fine-grained language changes. We describe the design and implementation of Helvetia and Language Boxes, discuss the required infrastructure of a host language enabling language embedding, and validate our approach by case studies that demonstrate different ways to extend or adapt the host language syntax and semantics.

Contents

List of Figures

List of Tables

Chapter 1

Introduction

"It might seem easy enough, but computer language design is just like a stroll in the park. Jurassic Park, that is."

— Larry Wall

General-purpose languages (GPLs), by being "good enough" to code software for arbitrary domains, are necessarily suboptimal for many specialized domains. They may be overly verbose, confusing or just plain awkward to use. Thus domain-specific languages (DSLs) have been developed to address the needs of these specialized domains.

DSLs come in three flavors: internal, external, and embedded. Table 1.1 summarizes their most important properties:

Internal Language. At one extreme we have the so-called internal languages which simply make creative use of APIs and of the host syntax. Such DSLs are sometimes referred to as *fluent interfaces* [Fowler, 2005a]. They provide a seamless integration in the host language, and as such they can benefit from the tools provided by the development environment (*e.g.*, code editor, debugger) of the host language. However, the expressiveness of internal DSLs is confined by the host syntax. In most programming languages it is possible to change neither the syntax nor the semantics of the host language.

External Language. At the other extreme we find external languages [Fowler, 2005b]. These languages are typically developed independently of the host language as a preprocessing step or through an extensible compiler. External languages provide freedom for expressing diverse syntax and semantics.

	Syntax	Semantics	Host Integration	Tool Integration	Description
Internal	○	○	●	●	Internal languages make a creative use of the host language. They integrate seamlessly into the host language and tools, but their syntax and semantics is strictly constrained.
External	●	●	○	○	External languages are independent of the host language. This makes them difficult to integrate into the host language and development tools.
Embedded	●	●	●	●	Embedded languages combine the advantages of internal and external languages. Ideally an embedded language uses the same executable representation as the host and integrates well with tools.

Table 1.1: Taxonomy for internal, external and embedded Languages.

While doing so they however break the tools of the host development environment. Integration with the host language is difficult.

Embedded Language. In between these two extremes we find embedded languages [Hudak, 1996], which extend a host language with new syntax and semantics. Language workbenches support the development of embedded languages by introducing a common representation and by integrating multiple languages into a common toolset. For example, editors take advantage of the abstract language definitions and automatically provide syntax highlighting, auto-completion and error correction. Ideally, a single debugger can be used to step through pieces of code implemented in different languages.

We have focused our research on embedded languages because they combine the strength of both, internal and external languages. Mernik *et al.* [Mernik *et al.*, 2005] point out that embedded approaches lead to better reuse of existing host language features and tools, and significantly reduce development and training costs. In practice however, language workbenches do not leverage the existing tools but provide their own environment. Often they introduce a non-standard language representation and thus pose compatibility problems with existing code.

1.1 Types of Embedded Languages

The *syntax* of a programming language is concerned with the form and structure of a program; it is typically specified using a set of rules called the grammar. The *semantic* of a programming language describes the meaning of a program; it can be specified using various techniques, most often it is given through documentation, a reference implementation, or denotational semantics. Together syntax and semantic define a programming language [Watt, 1991].

The *vocabulary* of a programming language is not only given by its syntax, but also through software libraries. Often a standard library forms the body of words used in a programming language. Additional libraries provide services for specify tasks. The set of active libraries defines the vocabulary a developer can use.

We have defined a taxonomy of different types of embedded languages and we assess how well existing approaches support their development and integration with existing tools. We have adopted a terminology from natural languages enlisted in Table 1.2. In the domain of natural language, a "pidgin" is "a grammatically simplified form of a language used for communication between people not sharing a common language"; a "creole" is "a mother tongue formed from the contact of two languages through an earlier pidgin stage"; an "argot" is a "jargon or slang of a particular group or class" [Jewell and Abate, 2005].

	Syntax	Vocabulary	Semantics	Description
Pidgin	○	●	●	A pidgin is a simplified form of the host language. It introduces a new vocabulary and new semantics to the code.
Creole	●	●	●	A creole changes the syntax of the host language (and therefore also the vocabulary) and defines new semantics.
Argot	○	○	●	An argot changes the semantics of the existing language without affecting its syntax.

Table 1.2: Taxonomy for pidgin, creole and argot embedded languages.

Pidgin. A pidgin bends the syntax of the host language to extend its semantics [Spinellis, 2001]. This kind of embedded language reuses a limited part of the host syntax and combines it with a new vocabulary. In their simplest form pidgins can be implemented by interpreting host language features, such as literal arrays or strings. A well-known example is the format string of the `printf` function in the standard C library.

Creole. A creole introduces a completely new syntax by defining its own grammar and a custom transformation to the host language that defines the semantics. For example, LINQ [Meijer *et al.*, 2006] combines C# with a convenient syntax to access relational databases and process XML. Also parser generators such as ANTLR [Parr, 2007] can be considered creoles, although they are mostly implemented external to the host language.

Argot. An argot uses the existing host language syntax, but changes its semantics. An argot reinterprets the semantics of valid host language code, whereas pidgin code is only syntactically correct host code — it has meaning only for the pidgin. Argots are commonly used to implement new crosscutting language features, such as transactional memory or continuation-passing style, without the language user needing to be aware of the change. Macro systems and aspect-oriented frameworks are well-known mechanisms for changing the behavior of the host language without touching its syntax.

An embedded language must either introduce new syntax to the host language for the concepts it introduces (a creole), or it must adopt the host syntax as is. If the host syntax is reused, it must either be overloaded, reinterpreting the syntax in a novel way (pidgin), or it must alter the semantics of the host (argot).

Two other possible combinations of the attributes of our taxonomy are listed in Table 1.3. While internal languages are a special case of embedded languages they typically do not require special tool support and thus are not in the focus of this dissertation. Furthermore, we take the host language as given.

	Syntax	Vocabulary	Semantics	Description
Internal Language	○	●	○	Internal languages are confined by the host syntax; they make a creative use of the host language and define a new vocabulary.
Host Language	○	○	○	The host language is a general-purpose programming language typically following a language standard. Most languages have fixed syntax and semantics.

Table 1.3: The remaining possible combinations of Table 1.2.

We argue that the categorization of embedded languages into pidgin, creole and argot languages is complete. Aside from internal and host languages, the remaining other combinations change the syntax but let the semantics unchanged. This does not make sense, as new syntax cannot be defined without also specifying its semantics.

1.2 Shortcomings of Existing Approaches

Developing new languages is expensive and requires a lot of knowledge in language design [Hoare, 1973]. In this dissertation, we propose a novel approach to deal with the challenges of language embedding:

Pidgin, Creole and Argot Languages. A fully general approach to integrate new embedded languages into an existing host language and environment must support the three classes of embedded languages: pidgins, creoles and argots.

Multiple Context-Dependent Languages. It should be practicable to mix and match different language extensions with the host language. Switching between different languages should be possible at arbitrary points and not enforce the use of special syntactic markers. Language changes should be scopable and possible conflicts should be gracefully handled [Bravenboer and Visser, 2004].

Homogeneous Tool Support. To ease the development and use of embedded languages existing tools such as code browsers, editors, debuggers or source control systems should seamlessly continue to work. With little additional development effort it should be possible to tweak or replace the existing tools to provide an improved user experience for embedded languages [Hudak, 1998].

Homogeneous Code and Data Abstraction. The executable code of the host and the embedded languages should be the same. This makes it possible to use a common reflective API and enables tools such as debuggers to work on multiple languages. A common code representation also avoids unnecessary interpretation layers that might come at a high performance penalty. Furthermore, a common data representation enables to transparently pass values between different languages without expensive conversions [Mernik *et al.*, 2005].

Conventional Language and Tools. A conventional language and development environment should be leveraged as the host instead of introducing a new or derived one. This avoids compatibility problems with existing code and lets developers use their accustomed development tools.

1.3 Thesis Statement

Thesis

1.4 Our Solution in a Nutshell

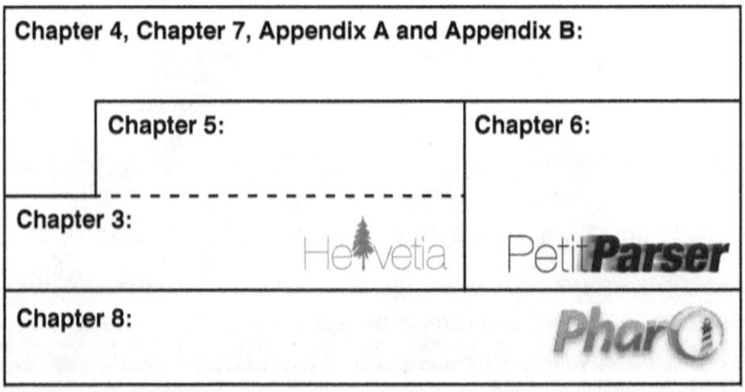

Chapter 4, Chapter 7, Appendix A and Appendix B:		
	Chapter 5:	Chapter 6:
Chapter 3:	Helvetia	Petit**Parser**
Chapter 8:		Phar

Figure 1.1:

Host Environment.

Helvetia System. The layer above the host environment is the core of the Helvetia system. This layer provides the necessary hooks into the host language compiler and the tools supplied with the development environment. Helvetia realizes an extensible rule engine to declaratively specify language and tool extensions. These rules can be seen as a macro language [Kohlbecker *et al.*, 1986] using reflection and pattern matching for scoping, and quasiquoting [Bawden, 1999] for code transformation and generation.

Language Boxes. Language Boxes are part of the Helvetia infrastructure and yield a simple model of modular and composable language extensions. Language Boxes work on a first-class grammar representation of the host language and thus abstract from the Helvetia rule model. *Language changes* are used to specify the composition of the host grammar together with the grammar of an embedded language. *Language concerns* denote a transformation from the embedded host language to the host language. Other concerns specify new behavior of the tools, such as syntax highlighting, contextual menus, error correction or autocompletion. The *language scopes* describe the contexts in which the new languages are enabled.

Dynamic Grammars. The mutable grammars provided by PetitParser is the enabling parser technology for Helvetia. We combine ideas from scannerless parsing [Visser, 1997], parser combinators [Hutton and Meijer, 1996], parsing expression grammars [Ford, 2004] and packrat parsers [Ford, 2002] to model grammars and parsers as objects that can be reconfigured dynamically.

Language and Tool Extensions. On the top layer are the language extensions. Language extension are either defined using modular Language Boxes or are directly described in terms of the Helvetia rule system. In both cases, the language and tool changes are specified uniformly using the Helvetia infrastructure.

1.5 Contributions

The main contributions of this dissertation are:

1. We present the *Helvetia* model which leverages the underlying representation of the host language to embed new languages into an existing host environment. Helvetia is an extensible system that intercepts the compilation pipeline of the host language and various tools such as editors and debuggers to seamlessly integrate language extensions. Helvetia provides a homo-

geneous language and tool integration into an existing host language [Renggli *et al.*, 2010c].

2. We propose the *Language Boxes* model, a modular mechanism to encapsulate (1) compositional changes to the host language, (2) transformations to address various concerns such as compilation and syntax highlighting, and (3) scoping rules to control visibility of fine-grained language extensions. Language boxes enable multiple context-dependent language extensions [Renggli *et al.*, 2009].

3. We demonstrate *PetitParser*, a dynamic grammar description framework. PetitParser makes it possible to dynamically transform, reuse, compose and extend language grammars as the enabling technology for Language Boxes [Renggli *et al.*, 2010b].

The following list details the contributions with some extended case studies, which serve as the validation of our approach:

Transactional Memory. Software transactional memory is an attractive mechanism for concurrency control, however it is difficult to integrate into existing languages and their tools. The use of Helvetia makes it possible to tightly integrate transactional semantics into an language without breaking existing tools [Renggli and Nierstrasz, 2009].

Code Quality. Domain-specific languages require domain-specific program checkers. We have applied the Helvetia infrastructure to detect common problems in domain-specific code and display and fix these problems using the existing infrastructure [Renggli *et al.*, 2010a].

Model Centric Transformations. Models of software structures are often far removed from the application domain. To enable dynamic adaptation of application logic we need to make application models more explicit in the code. The use of Helvetia made it possible to provide a fine-grained, context-dependent integration of models with application code [Nierstrasz *et al.*, 2009].

Host Language Choice. The Helvetia system is implemented in Smalltalk, a dynamic programming language. We have evaluated various general-purpose programming languages as the host environment and identified the key requirements to an environment to support Helvetia [Renggli and Gîrba, 2009].

1.6 Outline

The dissertation is structured as follows:

Chapter 2 discusses the related work of this thesis. We present various solutions to language embedding and analyze the five shortcomings in the context of each approach.

Chapter 3 introduces the Helvetia model and explains how the rule engine hooks into the compiler and the existing tools.

Chapter 4 validates the Helvetia model by demonstrating the implementation of real-world pidgin, creole and argot embedded languages.

Chapter 5 presents Language Boxes and describe how they enable modularity and a tight integration of multiple extensions with the host and other embedded languages.

Chapter 6 presents the dynamic grammar transformation infrastructure which is the enabling technology of Language Boxes.

Chapter 7 demonstrates the use of Helvetia for domain-specific program checking and automatic repair of violations.

Chapter 8 evaluated various host language choices and lists the key requirements for an implementation.

Chapter 9 concludes the dissertation and outlines future work.

Appendix A describes how to get started with Helvetia and gives an overview of how to implement first language extensions.

Appendix B gives an exhaustive list with additional pointers to embedded languages that we have built using Helvetia.

Chapter 2

Approaches for Combining Languages

> *"A programming language is a tool that has a profound influence on our thinking habits."*
>
> — Edsger Dijkstra

The history of domain-specific languages dates back to the early days of software engineering. One of the first domain-specific languages was the Backus–Naur Form (BNF) [Backus, 1959], a formal language to describe grammars. Over the years, various different terms have been used to describe domain-specific languages [Mernik *et al.*, 2005]: application-oriented languages [Sammet, 1969], special-purpose languages [Wexelblat, 1981], fourth-generation languages (4GL) [Martin, 1985], little languages [Bentley, 1986], and specialized languages [Bergin and Gibson, 1996].

The first one to define the term *domain-specific languages* was Lisa Walton [Walton, 1996]: "A Domain-Specific Language (DSL) is a small, usually declarative, language expressive over the distinguishing characteristics of a set of programs in a particular problem domain." Paul Hudak coined the term *embedded domain-specific languages* [Hudak, 1996] to refer to domain-specific languages that inherit the infrastructure of some other language.

In the 1990s there was considerable interest in the development of *architectural description languages* (ADLs) [Shaw and Garlan, 1996] to capture and express architectural knowledge of a software system. ADLs can be viewed as DSLs for describing the architecture of complex software systems. Many DSLs formalize architecture in terms of components, connectors, and the rules governing their composition [Shaw and Garlan, 1996]. This idea is also implicitly contained in the notion of *scripting languages*, which can be seen as DSLs for composing applications from components written in another, usually lower-level programming language [Ousterhout, 1998].

This interplay between conventional object-oriented languages, scripting languages and DSLs has been studied in the context of Piccola [Achermann *et al.*, 2001], a small language for composing applications from software components.

Unlike general-purpose programming languages, DSLs tend to be compact languages that provide appropriate notations and abstractions for a particular problem domain. It was shown that DSLs increase productivity and maintainability for specialized tasks [Deursen and Klint, 1997]. DSLs are often categorized as being either homogenous (internal), where the DSL uses the host language in an idiomatic way, or heterogeneous (external), where the two languages are distinct [Sheard, 2001]. Techniques are proposed to define language and semantics for new DSLs [Krahn *et al.*, 2007]. The idea of designing languages that embrace adding new DSLs has been a focus of research in the past [Odersky, 2007; Warth and Piumarta, 2007; Tratt, 2008]. However integrating those languages into existing tools has been largely neglected.

This chapter summarizes the state of the art in domain-specific language development. Section 2.1 summarizes on existing patterns for *internal languages*. Section 2.2 and Section 2.3 discusses tools and programming environments for development and use of *external* and *embedded languages*.

2.1 Internal Languages

Internal domain-specific languages have been widely popularized over the past years, although the underlying ideas are much older. Internal languages are easy to implement, because they make a creative use of APIs and often apply a subset of the host syntax only. As such an internal language can be freely intertwined with host language code. Existing tool facilities such as syntax highlighting, code folding, code completion, and debuggers mostly continue to work. The drawback of internal languages is that their expressiveness is confined by the syntax of the host language.

The literature mentions various patterns of building internal domain-specific languages, however there is no survey that consolidates all these patterns other than the draft of Fowler's DSL book [Fowler, 2010]. In the following paragraphs we present some of these patterns and demonstrate several examples. Furthermore we point out the weaknesses of these internal languages, to motivate the need for more powerful mechanisms. Table 2.1 lists these patterns and summarizes their applicability to various programming languages.

	C	C++	C#	Java	Javascript	Lisp	Haskell	Ruby	Smalltalk
2.1.1 Function Sequence	●	●	●	●	●	●	●	●	●
2.1.2 Function Nesting	●	●	●	●	●	●	●	●	●
2.1.3 Function Chaining	●	●	●	●	●	●	●	●	●
2.1.4 Higher-Order Functions	◐	◐	◐	◐	●	●	●	●	●
2.1.5 Language Literals	●	●	●	●	●	●	●	●	●
2.1.6 Operator Overloading	○	●	●	○	○	●	●	●	●
2.1.7 Meta-Annotations	○	○	●	●	○	◐	○	○	●
2.1.8 Program Generation	○	◐	◐	○	○	●	◐	○	◐
2.1.9 Macro Programming	◐	◐	○	○	○	●	◐	○	◐

Table 2.1: The applicability of various internal language patterns in common programming languages. ○ not supported, ◐ partly possible using workarounds, libraries or language extensions, ● full support.

2.1.1 Function Sequence

Function sequences are the most basic form of a DSL. A series of function calls is used to perform a sequence of actions or configuration steps. The functions that make up such an internal language are usually visible on a specific object or in a specific scope only, to avoid the pollution of the global namespace.

While function sequences are straightforward to implement in most languages, they show various limitations in practice. One such limitation is that the complete interface has to be implemented at a single place. Furthermore, if the language is used to describe something more than a flat list, then the implementation needs to keep track of a context. The Java example in Fowler's DSL book uses arbitrary whitespaces to visualize the nesting, this has however no meaning for the language itself:

```
computer();
   processor();
      cores(2);
      type(386);
   disk();
      size(150);
```

The Smalltalk programming language provides a unique syntactical construct called *cascade* that allows one to send multiple messages to the same receiver. This makes the function sequence a common pattern in Smalltalk. The Magritte metamodel

[Renggli *et al.*, 2007] uses cascades to configure its description objects with a sequence of configuration messages. The following example creates, configures and returns a description object for the attribute firstName of the class Person:

```
Person>>descriptionFirstName
    ^ MAStringDescription new
        accessor: #firstName;
        label: 'First Name';
        priority: 200;
        beRequired;
        yourself
```

2.1.2 Function Nesting

Nested function calls are similar to function sequences, but instead of sequencing the function calls they are nested as arguments to other calls. This gives the language developer more control as an implicit context is given through the call-stack. Furthermore a type system can reduce the possible valid calls at a given point in the source code. This variation of the previous pattern however does not solve the problem that all the functions need to be accessible globally.

To illustrate the function nesting Fowler adapts the example above:

```
computer(
    processor(
        cores(2),
        type(386)),
    disk(
        size(150)));
```

2.1.3 Function Chaining

A classical form of internal domain-specific languages is based on function chaining. Each function call returns a polymorphic receiver so that multiple operations can be performed on a single expression. Furthermore, functions can decide to return different objects depending on the context to change the active vocabulary. In statically typed languages this pattern allows IDEs to employ the type system to offer accurate completion actions. Possible candidate functions are not visible globally anymore but scoped to one or more objects.

A good example for function chaining is the jQuery Javascript library. The entry point to this query language is the global jQuery function. The example below starts a query in the context of the DOM elements that match the CSS query li. Note that this CSS selector is yet another kind of internal language, a literal language that we discuss in Section 2.1.5. The find function performs a new CSS query in the scope of the receiver and toggles the invisible class of the matching element. The end function closes this scope and slideToggle performs an animation on the original query result.

```
jQuery("li").find("span.active").toggleClass("invisible").end().slideToggle();
```

To make the scoping visually tangible function chains are often not formatted on a single line, but aligned depending on their scope. As Javascript (and Java) accepts arbitrary spaces between method invocations the above code can be formatted in a more readable way as below:

```
jQuery("li")
    .find("span.active")
        .toggleClass("invisible")
    .end()
    .slideToggle();
```

Method chaining can well be combined with other patterns for internal languages. The example below shows how the Java JMock framework [Freeman and Pryce, 2006] applies function sequence, function nesting and function chaining pattern:

```
offer = mock(Offer.class);
offer.expects(once())
        .method("buy")
        .with(eq(QUANTITY))
        .will(returnValue(receipt));
```

2.1.4 Higher-Order Functions

Higher-order functions can be composed to build new functions, passed as argument to other functions, and partially evaluated (curried) by providing arguments one at a time. Functional programming languages provide higher-order functions as their central concept, but in most other programming languages higher-order functions can be simulated using function pointers or function objects (C, Java). The use of higher-order functions is a popular technique to build internal domain-specific languages.

For example, parser combinator framework Parsec [Leijen and Meijer, 2001] (implemented in Haskell) uses function composition to build parsers. The example below composes the functions `many1` and `letter` and results in a function `word` that parses words. `many1` is a function that parses one or more occurrences of the function passed as argument. `letter` is a function that parsers a single letter.

```
word :: Parser String
word = many1 letter
```

Another example of an internal domain-specific language making use of higher-order functions is the Seaside web application framework [Ducasse *et al.*, 2007] (implemented in Smalltalk). Seaside does not use a templating engine to generate HTML code. Instead, a high-level interface reliefs developers from checking correct tag nesting and attributes. Block closures (higher-order functions) are used to define a domain-specific language for programmatic HTML generation.

The example below generates the HTML code `<div class="title"><h1>Domain-Specific Languages</h1><p>Nested Functions</p></div>`. Whenever a block is evaluated, the specified tag is opened, the content is generated and the tag is closed. Cascades are used to specify attributes on the tags. The current context is implicitly given through the stream variable `html`.

```
html div class: 'title'; with: [
   html heading
      level: 1;
      with: [ html text: self model title ].
   html paragraph
      with: [ html text: 'Nested Functions' ] ]
```

Higher-order functions are a good construct for internal languages, if the host language provides a simple construct for their creation. The square brackets in Smalltalk [...], the do ... end constructs in Ruby, the lambda (`lambda (...)` ...) constructs in Scheme and the inner functions in Javascript `function () { ... }` are concise.

In Java inner classes can be used to simulate higher-order functions, however they introduce a significant amount of clutter as multiple lines of code are required to define the class and open and close the block of code. A drawback of using higher-order functions is that they encapsulate their behavior and thus make it impossible to reflect and decompose their behavior after creation.

2.1.5 Language Literals

String literals and literal collections are a mechanism for realizing quick and dirty internal languages. A popular example is the `printf` function in C, which uses a string as the specification of how to format output:

```
char[] str = "World";
printf("Hello %s\n", str);                    /* prints "Hello World" */
```

Languages that support literal collections can go a step further and use those to define their own little languages. An example for such a language can be found in Smalltalk for the configuration of printing dates. The numbers and characters in the literal array define order of the different values, the characters that separate the different values and how the actual values are printed.

```
Date now print: aStream format: #(1 2 3 $  3 1)        " returns '15 March 2010' "
```

There are numerous potential problems when using language literals: As the literals are parsed and interpreted by a custom execution engine, developers have to implement a small interpreter that might have a bad performance. Also literals are limited in their expressiveness, users might have difficulties to integrate them in the system. Debugging is difficult, as the host language debugger will step through the interpreter instead of the application code. Additionally, errors are only detected at runtime, as compilers do not see the meaning behind the literals (most of today's C compilers check printf-strings though). Last, it is dangerous for a literal language to grow into a slow and buggy Lisp implementation[1].

2.1.6 Operator Overloading

Languages like C++, C#, Ruby, Python, Prolog, Haskell, and Smalltalk allow developers to implement or redefine custom operators. This is especially useful in a mathematical domain, because it makes custom data types (complex numbers, vectors or matrixes) look like the built-in types.

However, overloading operators has several problems, especially when the language restricts the operators to a predefined set. This is for example the case in C++, C#, Ruby, and Python. The use of operators outside their natural mathematical domain can cause confusion and bugs. For example the Standard Template Library

---

1 Greenspun's Tenth Rule of Programming: "Any sufficiently complicated C or Fortran program contains an ad-hoc, informally-specified bug-ridden slow implementation of half of Common Lisp." [http://philip.greenspun.com/research/]

(STL) in C++ has been criticized for using the shift operators << for streaming. In the expression s << 1 the static type of s determines if the built-in shift operation or the library function for streaming is called. Furthermore the hardcoded precedence of the operators can lead to unexpected results.

Prolog, Haskell and Smalltalk do not show the above problems. In these languages arbitrary new operators can be defined, so there is not necessarily a conflict of meaning with existing operators. In Prolog and Haskell the precedence of operators can be customized. In Smalltalk all operators have the same precedence and are always evaluated from left to right.

2.1.7 Meta-Annotations

Another popular way of specifying domain-specific concerns are annotations. For example, the Java testing framework JUnit 4 [Hunt and Thomas, 2003] uses a small set of annotations to declare test methods and specify various arguments.

In the following example the method addMoney is identified as a test method using the @Test annotation. Furthermore, the test is configured to fail if execution takes longer than 100 milliseconds:

```
@Test(timeout=100)
public void addMoney() {
    Money m12CHF = new Money(12, "CHF");
    Money m14CHF = new Money(14, "CHF");
    ...
```

JExample extends JUnit with explicit dependency information between tests cases [Kuhn *et al.*, 2008]. This enables tools to directly localize most relevant defects. The dependencies are declared using the @depends annotation as demonstrated in the following test excerpt:

```
@Test
@Depends("testPush")
public Stack testPop(Stack stack) {
    Object top = stack.pop();
    ...
```

While meta-annotations are supported in many today's programming language, the above examples also demonstrate their limitations. Typically annotations do not contain arbitrary host language expressions, but are limited to literal types and constants as arguments. In the example above we see that the dependent test method `testPush` is referenced using a string and not using a first-class reference. This can pose problems when code is refactored. Furthermore meta-annotations, as their name suggests, are generally not useful to describe sequence or flow. Annotations in Java can only be attached to structural members of the host language like packages, classes, methods, variables, etc. Annotations are queried and processed at runtime using a reflective API.

2.1.8 Program Generation

Multi-stage programming is a paradigm for runtime program generation [Taha, 2003; Calcagno *et al.*, 2003]. Multi-stage programs are generic and can be parametrized without unnecessary runtime overhead. In MetaOCaml the type system ensures at compile-time that dynamically generated programs are type-safe and require no additional checks later on. MetaOCaml adds syntactic constructs to OCaml for building, combining, and executing staged expressions.

Partial evaluation is a paradigm to create highly specialized code for program optimization and to change the program interpretation at compile-time [Jones *et al.*, 1993; Futamura, 1999]. Partial evaluation allows compilers to precompute static data and thus to avoid unnecessary calculations at runtime. For example, partial evaluation can be used to instantiate an interpreter with a program yielding an optimized implementation of the program.

Quoting mechanisms are available in programming languages like Scheme, Lisp, Template Haskell and MetaOCaml [Bawden, 1999]. Quoting provides the syntactic sugar for the implementation of multi-stage and partially evaluating programming languages:

For example, in Scheme the expression (+ 1 2) is evaluated to 3. In contrast, the quasiquoted expression `(+ 1 2) evaluates to the AST of the expression (+ 1 2). This quoted expression is not immediately executed, but instead can be used for code generation, code transformation or can be evaluated using an alternative evaluation strategy. In addition languages like Scheme provide syntax to unquote expressions. An unquoted expression is used within a quasiquoted expression and executed when the AST is built. It can be used to combine smaller quasiquoted expressions to larger ones. Last but not least, splices are expressions evaluated at compile-time and inserted into the AST before compilation.

```
> `(+ 1 2)                                              # quasiquote
(+ 1 2)
> `(+ 1 ,(+ 1 1))                                       # quasiquote + unquote
(+ 1 2)
> `(+ ,@(list 1 2))                                     # quasiquote + splice
(+ 1 2)
```

C# 3.0 introduces *expression trees* that represent code in a tree-like data structure. Rather than compiling a lambda expression into its executable form, the C# compiler creates a composite of expression nodes instead. The following two declarations define respectively a lambda function that can be normally evaluated and an expression tree of the same function that is a composite structure of expression objects:

```
Func<int, int> dup = x => 2 * x;
Expression<Func<int, int>> exprDup = x => 2 * x;
```

Expression trees are useful because they can be interpreted in various ways. For example, LINQ (Language Integrated Query) [Meijer *et al.*, 2006] uses expression trees to build SQL and XML queries from C# code. This has the advantage that syntax errors can be avoided at compile-time and that queries are statically typed together with the rest of the code. C# expression trees are not available reflectively on arbitrary expressions, but only for statically declared expressions defined at compile-time. Furthermore, C# does not make it possible to encode sequences of statements, only simple expressions are supported.

2.1.9 Macro Programming

Programming languages like Lisp, Dylan, Scheme and Clojure have sophisticated macro systems giving developers the possibility to transform the program structure using the quoting techniques described in Section 2.1.8. While in Lisp and Clojure macros are used to explicitly constructs parts of a program, in Dylan and Scheme a pattern matching algorithm is used to replace matching parts of the program with a transformed form. In both cases it is possible to change the default evaluation rules of code and to build simple literal languages that are automatically transformed to executable code.

Macros alone do not allow the syntax to be changed. In Lisp reader macros can be used to introduce custom parsers that transform arbitrary input into code the Lisp compiler can understand. An example of a reader macro can be found in the

XMLisp library [Repenning and Ioannidou, 2009]. XMLisp allows developers to paste verbatim XML directly into Lisp code without having to worry about escaping issues that would arise from including it as a string.

```
; an XML string without reader-macros
(setq anchor-plainlisp "<a href=\"http://scg.unibe.ch/\">SCG</a>")


(setq anchor-xmlisp <a href="http://scg.unibe.ch/">SCG</a>)
```

Reader macros are not that well known in the community and as widely applied as one could expect. Partial evaluation, macro programming and reader macros are powerful mechanisms to implement internal domain-specific languages that do not break the tools. Unfortunately these techniques are not supported by most mainstream programming languages and are considered hard to understand even by experienced developers.

2.2 External Languages

External languages are less interesting in our context. Integration of the host environment and the external language is difficult at best. In most cases data needs to be converted when being passed back and forth between the external language and the host environment. Dedicated development tools for external languages are often not available or separate from the host language tools.

Typical examples of external languages are Unix tools like *grep*, *sed* and *awk* to process and filter data. Other unix tools solve very specific problems, such as *make* that topologically sorts and executes a graph of dependent tasks. Another common group includes external query languages:

- *Regular expressions* are used for matching strings using patterns of characters. Regular expressions are widely applied. Most programming languages provide implementations of regular expressions as part of their standard library (Java) or even have a special literal type for regular expressions in the language definition (Javascript, Ruby).

- *XPath* is a query language for XML documents. Most XML libraries provide facilities to pass an XPath query as a string and subsequently parse and process it on a given ML document. This wraps the external XPath language effectively into an internal literal language, as described in Section 2.1.5.

- *Structured Query Language* (SQL) and other data manipulation and query languages are used in most business applications. While it is still common practice to put SQL strings into the host language, various solutions have been introduced to remove the burden of specifying the external language from the developer. Object-relational mapping tools provide the infrastructure to convert data between object-oriented languages and relational database systems. For instance, Active Record enables Ruby developers to specify queries and simple database operations using an internal domain-specific language. Similarly LINQ provides a convenient syntax to query and transform both XML and SQL data-sources using the same internal language.

The development of external languages is not different from the development of a new general-purpose programming language. It involves specifying a grammar, generating or implementing a parser, and developing interpreter or compiler. These steps are complex and time-consuming because developers need to start from scratch. Often it is too expensive to build dedicated editors and debuggers.

2.3 Embedded Languages

Table 2.2 provides an overview of the related work split into four categories. For each system considered we indicate the host language, the capability of defining pidgins, creoles and argots, and the support for the aforementioned characteristics. The following sections offer details for each individual system.

2.3.1 Extensible Compilers

Extensible Compilers are best described as open toolboxes that provide entry points into the compiler toolchain to extend and change the host language.

ableJ [Van Wyk *et al.*, 2007], *Dryad* [Kats *et al.*, 2008], *JastAddJ* [Ekman and Hedin, 2007], and *Polyglot* [Nystrom *et al.*, 2003] are extensible Java compiler frameworks and provide the necessary infrastructure to build argots, pidgins and creoles. Language extensions are composable and modular, and are transformed into Java for execution. Most extensible compilers define the syntax changes using an external language definition. The Dryad compiler uses bytecode as its central representation, and thus it is not homogeneous as well. None of the systems offers IDE integration, and transformed code cannot be debugged at the source level.

The *Java Annotation Processing Tool* (APT) enables a compile-time, read-only view of the Java program structure. ASTs can be transformed only using a private API,

Type	System	Pidgin Languages	Creole Languages	Argot Languages	Multiple Context-Dependent Languages	Homogeneous Tool Support	Homogeneous Code and Data Abstraction	Conventional Language and Tools
2.3.1 Extensible Compilers	ableJ	●	●	●	●	○	○	●
	Dryad	●	●	●	●	○	○	●
	JastAddJ	●	●	●	●	○	○	●
	Polyglot	●	●	●	●	○	●	●
	Java Annotation Processing	●	○	●	●	○	●	●
	Xoc	●	●	●	●	○	○	●
2.3.2 Meta-Programming Systems	Cola	○	●	○	●	○	●	○
	Converge	○	●	○	●	○	●	○
	MetaOCaml	●	○	●	●	○	●	●
	Scheme	●	○	●	●	●	●	●
2.3.3 Language Workbenches	JetBrains MPS	○	●	○	●	●	●	○
	Intentional Software	●	●	●	●	●	●	○
	openArchitectureWare	○	●	○	○	○	○	●
	WholePlatform	○	●	○	○	○	○	●
	Xtext	○	●	○	○	●	○	●
	Java Development Tools	○	○	○	○	●	○	●
	IDE Metatooling Platform	○	○	○	○	●	○	●
	Katahdin	○	●	○	●	○	●	○
	Ceteva XMF	○	●	○	●	○	●	○
2.3.4 Language Transformations	Khepera	●	●	●	○	○	○	●
	TXL	○	●	○	○	○	○	○
	ASF+SDF	○	●	○	●	○	○	○
	MontiCore	○	●	○	○	○	○	●
	MetaBorg	●	●	●	●	○	○	●
	Linglet Transformation System	○	●	○	○	○	●	●
	Java Language Extender	○	●	○	○	○	○	●
2.3.5 Modeling Languages	Xactium	○	○	○	○	○	●	○
	Kermeta	○	○	○	○	○	●	○
	MetaEdit+	○	○	○	○	○	○	○
	Software Factories	○	○	○	○	○	○	○

Table 2.2: Comparison of different systems for language authoring.

which is not supported and may be subject to change or deletion. As such, argots and pidgins can be implemented, but a creole would require an additional preprocessing step. In a similar way people are using the weaving mechanism of AOP to achieve semantic changes for pidgins and argots.

Xoc [Cox *et al.*, 2008] is an extensible C compiler. Xoc uses a source-to-source translator that reads the input, analyzes and transforms it, to eventually generate standard C code. The system provides no reflective facilities and no tool integration, neither at compile-time nor at runtime.

2.3.2 Meta-Programming Systems

Meta-Programming Systems are programming languages based on meta-programming facilities targeted at code generation.   Systems like the ones described here support program generation and macro programming as presented in Section 2.1.8 and Section 2.1.9.

Cola [Piumarta and Warth, 2006] implements an open object model for experimentation with different programming paradigms. Cola is bootstrapped in itself using a Smalltalk-like language called Pepsi. Jolt is a Lisp-like language that serves as a common abstract syntax and executable representation for other languages. OMeta [Warth and Piumarta, 2007] is an object-oriented pattern matcher based on Parsing Expression Grammars that is used to transform new languages to Jolt. Even if all languages are built on top of the same infrastructure, the authors do not provide mechanisms to easily embed them into each other. Furthermore there is no common tool support for editing and debugging the different languages.

Converge [Tratt, 2005] is a dynamic programming language resembling Python. A special block construct `$<<language>>` is used to embed languages into the source code. The modification or extension of existing languages is not possible, thus argots and pidgins cannot be created. Meta-programming is possible at compile-time only. There is no IDE integration.

MetaOCaml [Calcagno *et al.*, 2003] uses multi-stage programming to generate and transform code at runtime. Similar quoting mechanisms are available in programming languages like *Scheme*, Lisp or Template Haskell, but these mechanisms alone do not permit new syntax to be introduced. Both system have powerful macro programming constructs, making it possible to tweak the default towards pidgins or argots. Typically these kinds of systems are used together with traditional text editors and thus do not allow an easy adaptation to language changes. Debuggers are available.

2.3.3 Language Workbenches

Language Workbenches [Fowler, 2005b] are characterized by a specialized IDE with a well-defined workflow to specify and use different languages. Language designers are required to follow clearly defined steps to describe syntax, semantics and editor behavior of a new language.

The *Meta Programming System* (MPS) by JetBrains [Dimitriev, 2004] and *Intentional Software* [Simonyi et al., 2006] both provide a programming environment to define new languages and to change existing ones. Neither system uses text representation for source code, but instead they provide a graphical cell editor that maps valid programs directly to an underlying abstract code representation. MPS defines new languages using different concepts for structure (semantic model), editor (parser), constraints, behavior, type systems, data flow and code generators for Java. MPS 1.1 does not come with a source level debugger; debugging and error reporting happens at the level of the generated Java code. Similarly Intentional Software requires language developers to define, edit, display and transform concerns for language extensions. As no product previews and no detailed documentation are available, the exact properties of this system are not clear.

openArchitectureWare and *Whole Platform* [Solmi, 2005] are language workbenches that are tightly integrated into the Eclipse platform. In both cases templating systems are used to generate executable Java code. openArchitectureWare provides a strong integration with the Eclipse meta-modeling facilities, such as the Eclipse Modeling Framework (EMF) and the Graphical Modeling Framework (GMF). They both provide basic support for editor integration such as syntax highlighting and code completion of textual languages. However, both systems lack debugging support and the ability to change the semantics of their host language.

Xtext is a framework for development of textual domain-specific languages. It is integrated well with the Eclipse environment and especially the Eclipse modeling tools. It does not provide the possibility to change the Java programming language itself though.

The *Java Development Tools* (JDT) provide the basic tools to build Eclipse plugins. The *IDE Metatooling Platform* (IMP) [Charles et al., 2009] is an extensible IDE architecture for the Eclipse platform. Contrary to all other tools listed in this section JDT and IMP do not provide functionality for language design and embedding themselves. The only purpose of IMP is to closely integrate existing languages into the Eclipse IDE using a service architecture. At the time being there is no support for interaction with language runtimes and debuggers.

Katahdin [Seaton, 2007] is a programming language implemented on top of C#. Katahdin is a dynamically typed language that syntactically resembles C#. New constructs such as expressions or statements are defined by subclassing existing parse-tree nodes that can then be added to the host language at runtime. Languages can be enabled on a per-file basis or can be integrated into the host language by extending it with a specific keyword such as `language { ... }` and connecting the two grammar-trees. The semantics of user-defined parse-tree nodes is specified by overriding certain methods in the respective node-classes. Code is interpreted by traversing the parse-tree nodes and calling methods defining the semantics. There is a simple debugger available visualizing the internal parse-tree structure of the interpreter. The debugger is not able to work at the level of Katahdin programs.

The Extensible Programming Language (XMF) by Ceteva is a specification of a "superlanguage" [Clark *et al.*, 2008]. A superlanguage is characterized through usability (interactive, dynamic, reflection, interfaces), expressiveness (high-level, dynamic typing, garbage-collection) and extensibility (aspects, reflexive, extensible-syntax). XMF is written in itself and allows one to easily define new languages. A special `@language` construct is used to switch between different languages. Although a Java interface is available, XMF uses its own proprietary virtual machine written in Java. XMF does not provide an IDE integration.

2.3.4 Language Transformations

Language transformation systems define languages through the transformation and composition of language models.

Khepera [Faith *et al.*, 1997] is a preprocessor that transforms source-to-source and pretty-prints the generated code to C before compiling with a traditional compiler. It parses input into an abstract syntax tree and performing complex tree-based analysis and manipulation. All transformations preserve the knowledge of the origin of each node. Thus, in theory Khepera makes it possible to develop debuggers for new languages. However, the system provides no ready-to-use IDE or debugger. Furthermore, it does not support multiple languages to be used simultaneously.

TXL [Cordy, 2006] is a source transformation system for experimentation with language design. A TXL program consists of a base grammar definition and a series of overrides that extend and change the base grammar. While various traversal and rewrite strategies can be contextually scoped to perform a source-to-source transformation it is not possible to change the grammar definition on-the-fly. Our model provides a high-level concept of language changes that are augmented with different transformation concerns for compiler and tool integration. Our target is always the host language AST, which is directly used to generate executable code.

ASF+SDF [Klint, 1993] is a language neutral collection of tools for the interactive construction of language definitions and associated tools. SDF is implemented as a scannerless generalized LR parser and supports the composition of grammars. A single parse table is created for all possibly active productions, and depending on the context the corresponding transitions are enabled and disabled. Our use of parser combinators allows us to directly model the grammar as an executable graph of productions that can be recombined and modified on the fly.

MontiCore [Krahn *et al.*, 2008] provides a framework for language inheritance and language embedding. MontiCore has its own syntax to define grammars and their mapping to Java types. The parser is created using the ANTLR [Parr, 2007] parser generator. The abstract syntax tree is automatically derived from the grammar. Language inheritance allows one to subclass existing grammars to modify and extend. Language embedding is achieved by manually introducing a superordinate parser for every pair of languages that are used together. ANTLR has been extended to support swapping between the grammars on the fly. Visitors are used to add new behavior for productions to generate code and to build editors for Eclipse. There is no IDE integration or support for debugging.

MetaBorg [Bravenboer and Visser, 2004] is a method for embedding DSLs and extending existing languages. MetaBorg is based on the *Stratego/XT* [Visser, 2004] toolkit, a language independent program transformation engine. MetaBorg employs a scannerless generalized LR parser technique to compose different grammars and an annotated term language to build abstract syntax trees. While this approach is language independent, it is also much more complex than our implementation. Our use of a parser combinator library makes it straightforward to define and transform arbitrary context-free grammars; ambiguities are supported and automatically resolved by the rule order. To define the transformation, MetaBorg uses a quoting mechanism, however the resulting code is pretty printed to a string before passing it on to the compiler of the host language. Hence there is no close integration in the compiler, the development environment or code debuggers.

The *Linglet Transformation System* [Cleenewerck, 2003] provides a mechanism to modularize the syntax and semantics of a single language construct. The code to generate is specified using a templating system. Linglets can be composed with each other and integrated into the host language at specific extension points. There is no support to replace or change existing language features and no scoping mechanism. Contrary to our approach, the linglets are only used during compilation; other tools do not take advantage of the language model.

Van Wyk *et al.* [Van Wyk *et al.*, 2002] propose forwarding attribute grammars to catalyze modularity of language extensions. The *Java Language Extender* framework [Van Wyk *et al.*, 2007] is the tool that uses this technique to import domain-adapted languages into Java. The use of LR-style parsers enforces certain restrictions to imported extensions, as the resulting grammar needs to be unambiguous. Language extensions can be scoped to files, but not at a more fine-grained scale. The Java Language Extender framework does not provide an integration into the IDE.

2.3.5 Modeling Languages

Muller *et al.* [Muller *et al.*, 2005b] present a specific metamodel and associated DSL for the modeling of dynamic web specific concerns. Web applications are represented as three related models (business, hypertext and presentation). To specify constraints and behavior on the model, an action language (based on OCL and Java) is used. *Xactium* [Clark *et al.*, 2004] and *Kermeta* [Muller *et al.*, 2005a] are executable meta-languages that define new languages similar to work with EMOF [Group, 2004]. Both provide a dedicated language for specifying meta-level operations, however they lack appropriate tool support.

MetaEdit+ [Tolvanen *et al.*, 2007] and *Software Factories* [Greenfield and Short, 2003] focus on domain-specific modeling. Both are interactive environments for defining graphical models and metamodels. Executable code, constraint checkers, and documentation can be generated through user-defined model-to-code transformations. MetaEdit+ is language-independent and thus provides only a debugger for the code generator. Software Factories transforms to C# code and is closely integrated with Microsoft VisualStudio.

2.4 Roadmap

In this chapter we reviewed the state of the art of language embedding.

Internal languages are a viable option in most general-purpose programming languages. Internal languages provide a tight integration into the host language; they do not break existing tools and passing data back and forth is trivial. However, internal languages do have limits. An internal language is strictly bound to the syntax and semantics the host language provides. In most of today's programming languages it is not possible to implement pidgin, creole and argot languages.

External languages are open and give a lot of freedom to the developer, however come at a high price. A complete language needs to be designed and implemented from scratch. Furthermore, tool support and the integration with a general-purpose language requires the attention of the developer. In many cases an external language is a requirement, because problem domains cannot be expressed adequately using internal languages.

Embedded languages try to combine the best properties of internal and external languages. As such, they enable developers to build their own languages while at the same time provide a tight embedding into a host environment. In Section 2.3 we reviewed existing approaches and we summarized their shortcomings in Table 2.2. The shortcomings introduced in Section 1.2 form the open challenges of a novel approach:

- A general approach to language embedding should support *pidgin, creole and argot languages*;

- It should be possible to arbitrarily mix and match *multiple context-dependent languages*;

- *Homogeneous tool support* should make it possible to reuse and adapt existing tools of the host language;

- *Homogeneous code and data abstractions* should avoid unnecessary interpretation layers and allow users to transparently pass data around; and

- A *conventional environment* should be leveraged to avoid compatibility problems with existing code.

In Chapter 3 we present the Helvetia model, the infrastructure for homogeneous tool and language integration in a conventional host language. Chapter 4 details how the Helvetia model provides support for the implementation of pidgin, creole and argot languages. In Chapter 5 and Chapter 6 we present the Language Box model that provides a modular mechanism for tightly intermixed language extensions. Figure 2.1 displays schematically the chapters and the problem space they cover.

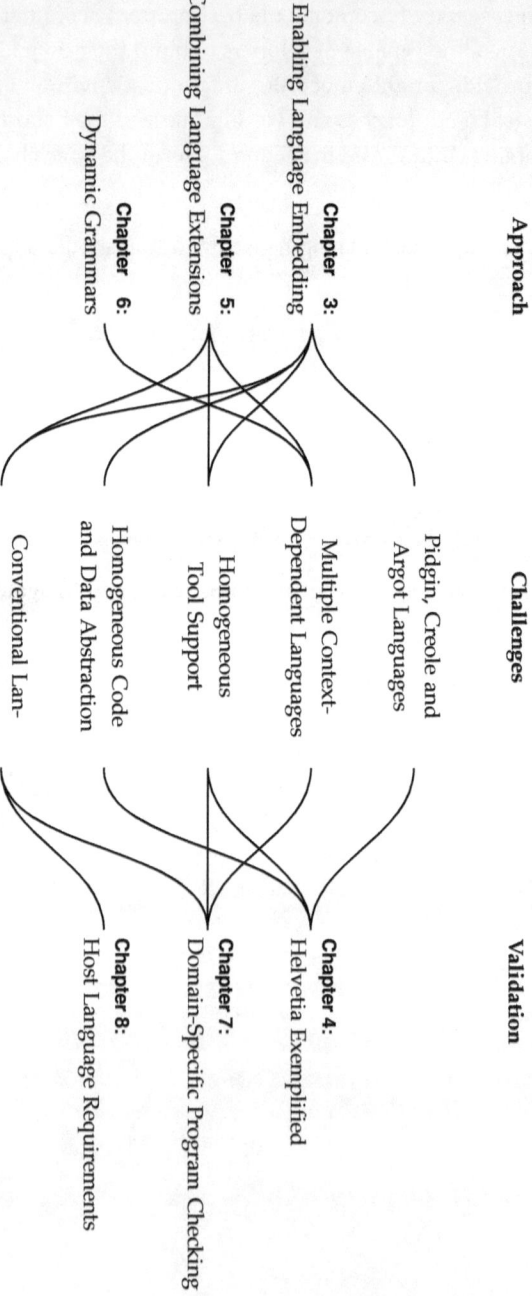

Figure 2.1: Structure of the dissertation and how it covers the problem space.

Chapter 3

Enabling Language Embedding

"Language designers are not intellectuals. They're not as interested in thinking as you might hope. They just want to get a language done and start using it."

— Dave Moon

In this chapter we present Helvetia[1], an extensible development environment for defining embedded languages and for integrating these languages into the tools of an existing host language. Helvetia accommodates new languages through extension points of the existing compiler and tools. All languages are transformed to the abstract syntax tree (AST) of the host language. These transformations are expressed as rules and they can be scoped to various contexts. Furthermore, these rules can be active at the same time, allowing us to embed different languages into a common host language, and to integrate them into the host environment and its tools.

3.1 The Helvetia Model

Our approach builds on top of the existing infrastructure of the host language, while existing tools — such as editors and debuggers — continue to work with minimal adaptation. Helvetia provides the necessary low-level infrastructure for *Language Boxes*, an adaptive language model for fine-grained language changes and language composition discussed in Chapter 5.

---

1 Helvetia is the Latin name of Switzerland. Its four official languages are French, German, Italian, and Romansh. We imagine the Helvetia system to be an environment where different languages can reuse the same infrastructure and be tightly interconnected as is the case in Switzerland.

Helvetia provides a *macro system* for a high-level programming language that goes beyond changing syntax and semantics only, but that also enables language designers to adapt tools. Helvetia uses the reflective facilities of the host language and parse-tree pattern matching to identify the elements of a transformation.

Transformations can be specified declaratively or imperatively. Either way, transformations preserve the mapping from the original source code to the executable code representation. This enables debuggers to know the current execution point in the untransformed source code. Thus, the source code, the abstract code representation and the executable code are causally connected. Furthermore, there is no added interpretative overhead as all behavior is compiled down to the native code representation of the host language.

3.1.1 Homogeneous Language Integration

Helvetia integrates multiple embedded languages with existing tools by leveraging and intercepting the existing toolchain and the underlying representation of the host language. Helvetia provides hooks to intercept parsing, AST transformation and semantic analysis of the standard compilation toolchain.

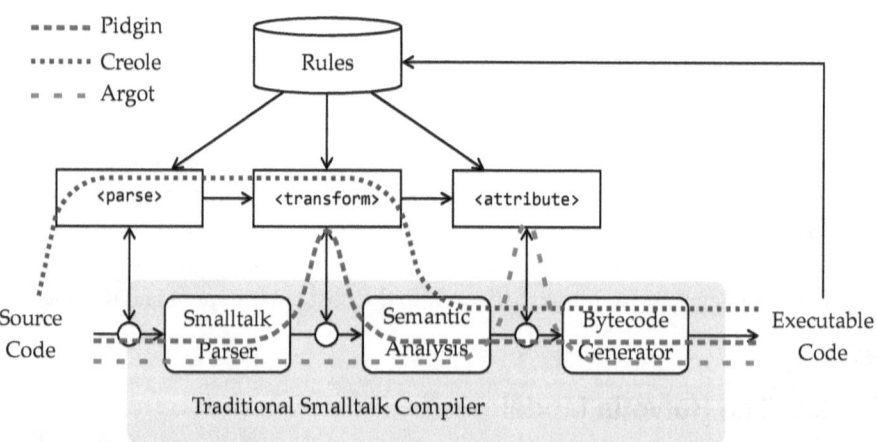

Figure 3.1: The code compilation pipeline showing multiple interception paths: Helvetia provides hooks to intercept parsing <parse>, AST transformation <transform> and semantic analysis <attribute>.

Whenever a source artifact is compiled the standard host language compiler consults the Helvetia rule engine before and after each compilation step. As depicted in Figure 3.1 this enables us to intercept and modify the data passed from one step to the other. We are able to perform source-to-source transformations or to bypass the regular parser altogether. Furthermore, we are able to perform AST transformations either before, instead of, or after semantic analysis.

The rules to intercept this transformation pipeline are defined using annotated methods. These methods constitute conventional Smalltalk code that is called at compile-time [Tratt, 2008]. The interception rules enable us not only to modify data in the pipeline but also to bypass conventional components.

- A rule marked with `<parser>` allows one to intercept the parsing of the source code. The result of a parser rule can be either a new source string (in case of a source-to-source transformation) or a Smalltalk AST (in which the original parser is skipped).

- A rule marked with `<transform>` is performed on the AST after parsing and before semantic analysis. It allows developers to apply arbitrary transformations on the AST. Furthermore, it is possible to change the default semantic analysis and instead perform a custom one.

- A rule marked with `<attribute>` is performed after symbol resolution and before bytecode generation. This permits to perform transformations on the attributed AST as well.

The Helvetia rules form a rewriting system for strings and terms [Baader and Nipkow, 1998]. Rules typically consist of two parts: the first part defines a pattern to match on the input; and the second part defines a transformation on the matched input. The details of how patterns and transformations are specified are discussed in Section 3.1.3.

Compilation errors are handled by the standard toolchain. Since all data passed from one step to the next carries information on its original source location, the error location is determined automatically and it is revealed to the user through the traditional means of the compiler. When a variable is undeclared, its occurrence is highlighted and the user is asked to correct the problem.

Since all rules are implemented within the host language, it is possible to span new compilation processes (local-to-global transformations) or cancel the current compilation process at any point. This is useful when the compilation of a single method results in the creation of multiple methods. Similarly it is possible for different methods to compile down to a single executable method of the underlying language (global-to-local transformations). This is useful when different methods are in-lined or combined for optimization purposes.

Source-position information is automatically tracked throughout the compilation chain to enable debugging for different languages. Furthermore, Helvetia uses the same rule infrastructure to extend and change how code browsers and editors work.

This allows one to introduce custom highlighting, code completion and contextual actions in a similar way as we will see in the next section.

3.1.2 Homogeneous Tool Integration

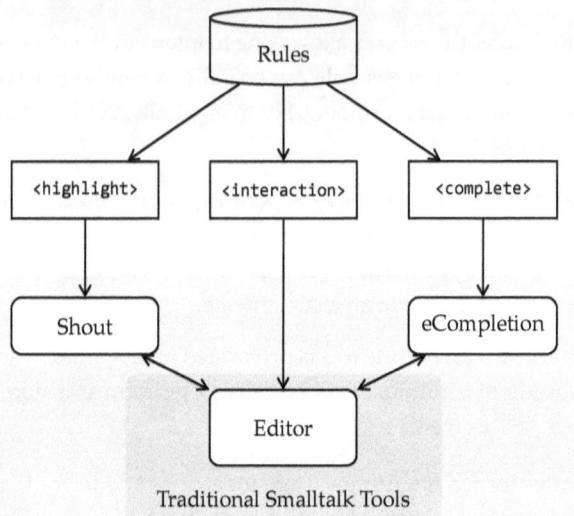

Figure 3.2: The tool integration with multiple extension points.

Figure 3.2 depicts the integration of the Helvetia rule system into the editor framework of our host environment. The traditional syntax highlighter *Shout* and the code completer *eCompletion* are themselves extensions to the basic code editing facilities. We changed their implementation and the editor itself to consult the rule database for customizable operations.

For example, to control syntax highlighting a rule can change the default highlighting. The traditional Smalltalk syntax highlighter is only applied to normal Smalltalk methods. As soon as there is a custom parser involved, the affected part of the source code remains black unless a custom highlighter is provided. The annotation `<highlight>` is used to define a highlighting rule. Helvetia provides similar extension points for code-completion and contextual menus.

Without introducing dedicated editors Helvetia nicely blends into the existing programming environment. For example looking for class references, senders or implementors of a method works transparently and exactly as the developer would expect. This is because these queries are implemented on the abstract code representation of the system. Custom interaction blocks can be provided through the `<interaction>` annotation.

The lack of dedicated tools to find and fix bugs in a new language is one of the major drawbacks when designing and using embedded languages. Since our approach uses the code abstraction of the host language, the standard debugging tools continue to work. One can set breakpoints as in conventional methods. Stepping through code written in a mixture of languages poses no problem either. The AST of a debugged method carries information about the source range in the original code. Generated code either reuses the source ranges of the parent node, or has no source range and is therefore invisible in the debugger. With this information from the original AST the debugger is able to accurately highlight the current execution point and step to the next statement, without having to know anything about the structure of the source string.

Our current Helvetia implementation does not change the way the debugger presents information, *e.g.*, the stack frames and variables are displayed at the level of host language. However, we envision the addition of new rules to enable the customization of the debugger's user-interface. Inspecting and changing intermediate values is equally possible. Changing and recompiling the source code on the fly from within the debugger is possible too, this being an inherited feature of the host language.

By default the debugger does not display code transformations, but shows the original-source code and highlights the execution location. Language developers however have the possibility to change the view in the debugger and instead display the transformed source code. This is possible because we remember the original and transformed AST nodes and their respective mapping to bytecode with every compiled method.

3.1.3 Defining Helvetia Rules

Helvetia uses *annotated methods* on the class-side (static) to define a rule database that is queried by the compiler and other tools. The rules affect instance-code of the corresponding class and its subclasses. To define a system-wide rule, it has to be installed within an extension method for `Object`, the root of the class hierarchy.

The following primitive rule types are currently supported:

- The `ConditionRule` behaves like a case statement. An ordered list of conditions is checked and the first matching action is executed. If no match is found a default action is executed as an alternative. The condition is implemented using the host language and can perform arbitrary checks using the reflective

API of the host language. This rule type is typically used to further scope the effect of rules to specific parts of the system. This rule type can be used with any input.

- `MatchRule` and `RangeRule` use regular expressions to match source code. This is useful to check for specific strings in the code when no parse-tree is available yet. For example, regular expressions are sometimes used to provide custom syntax highlighting within string literals of the host language. In many cases matching the parse-tree is simpler. This rule type is only supported for rules that take text as input, for example `<parse>`.

- The `TreeRule` is a parse-tree matcher. Unlike string matching these patterns work on the AST and make it possible to efficiently find all occurrences of particular node combinations. Again, action code can be supplied that is executed when a match is found. This rule type is only supported for rules that take an AST as input, for example `<transform>` and `<attribute>`.

Rules can be arbitrarily nested. Instead of attaching host language code to perform a transformation, another rule can be used that is subsequently applied in the context of the parent match. Furthermore it is possible to supply a custom rule object such as a custom parser or syntax highlighter.

3.2 Evaluation of the Helvetia Model

In Section 2.3 we presented various approaches to language embedding. In this section we compare the approach of Helvetia with the existing solutions summarized in Table 2.2.

3.2.1 Pidgin, Creole and Argot Languages

In the related work, support for pidgin, creole and argot embedded languages is variable. In the category of extensible compilers usually all types are supported. Meta-programming systems either do not provide a model of the host language that can be modified (Converge) or do not provide the possibility to change the syntax (MetaOCaml, Scheme). Language workbenches are designed to implement creoles, that is to build new language elements and combine them with other languages.

3.2.2 Multiple Context-Dependent Languages

The integration of new embedded languages into each other and into the host language is solved in different ways. Many existing approaches provide a very coarse-grained control and allow one to change the language on a per-file basis only. Other systems give a more fine-grained control but require special tokens to switch between languages (Converge and XMF). In Katahdin this token is freely definable by changing the host language.

In Helvetia the scope of each language is defined in a way that differs from the systems discussed. Language extensions are defined in rules that use reflection capabilities of the host language to check for specific conditions. Namespaces, packages, class-hierarchies, or annotated classes can define a scope. At a method level we are able to look for specific annotations in the source string or simply try different parsers. At a sub-method level we are able to look for certain code statements to transform, either using regular-expressions (before parsing) or using parse-tree matching (after parsing). These techniques enable a fine-grained control over the languages, however for end users it is often less evident, what parts of the system belong to the host language or are externally defined. This can be addressed by means of tailored highlighting of such code.

Multiple rule-sets can be active at the same time. For example, both an argot and a creole can be active at the same time, since they do not perform transformations at the same place in the compiler toolchain. If conflicting rules are active, for instance two language extensions that define their own parser, Helvetia throws an error. We propose a solution for this limitation in Chapter 5.

Transformation rules typically do not conflict, since they work on the same AST model. Rules are performed in a deterministic order based on their priority. Thanks to the reflective capabilities of the system, each rule can detect other active rules and choose to disable itself or other rules on the fly. In practice conflicts are rare, because language extensions are typically scoped to a small portion of the system, such as a class hierarchy or a package.

3.2.3 Homogeneous Tool Support

Most systems provide debugging tools for language developers, however they mostly lack sophisticated debugging support for application developers. We believe that it is crucial for the end users of a language to have good debugging support. Implementing custom debuggers is expensive and thus seldom done in practice. Furthermore switching between different debuggers in a multilingual environment is cumbersome. End users do not want to be forced to learn new tools, but instead prefer the familiar tools provided by the host language in use.

Helvetia supports the use of the existing debugging facilities for language developers and end users. While the host language debugger might not offer the optimal abstraction for all languages, it offers a free live view on the untransformed source code and the current execution point. This is something that most other systems do not provide without additional development effort.

3.2.4 Homogeneous Code and Data Abstraction

Language transformation systems use a preprocessor. This considerably slows down the compile cycles, as several transformation passes and compilation cycles of different independent tools are involved. Furthermore, it can be difficult to debug the generated code, as it is often impossible to provide a correct mapping from generated code back to the original source. Different host and meta-languages make interoperability more difficult.

Helvetia maintains this mapping throughout a single compiler pipeline that allows one to use this information in the standard Smalltalk debugger. Transformation rules are defined in the host language and take advantage of the reflective capabilities of the system.

3.2.5 Conventional Language and Tools

Meta-programming systems and language workbenches provide large toolsets to define new languages, however in many cases (Converge, MPS, Intentional Software, Katahdin, XMF) they use derivatives. In a few cases (Katahdin, XMF) they implement a new runtime layer, which makes it difficult to reuse existing code and libraries. In other cases they build on top of existing languages and infrastructure (MetaOCaml, Scheme, openArchitectureWare, Xtext, Java Development Tools, IDE Metatooling Platform).

We believe that it is beneficial for the adaptation of a language authoring system to build into an existing host language and leverage as many features as possible. Helvetia reuses the host language code representation, the complete compiler toolchain and the existing IDE to provide a lightweight language integration. Helvetia code shows no performance penalty as it uses the same runtime infrastructure as the host language.

In Chapter 8 we will evaluate several other host language choices for a system like Helvetia. Smalltalk has proven to be a good practical choice for our prototype, though not a requirement:

- In Smalltalk the compiler is part of the development environment and can be changed on the fly. For Helvetia, we did so by carefully introducing interception points before and after the different compilation steps. Rules are defined using annotated methods that are evaluated at compilation time.

- Rules that work on AST nodes need to preserve the source mapping with every transformation. In our case we use a transformation system based on the refactoring engine of the host language. Meta-programming facilities such as parse-tree matching and quasiquoting greatly simplifies code transformation.

- As with the compiler, editors are required to support extension points for custom highlighting, code completion, error reporting, *etc.* In Smalltalk the editors are implemented within the host language and can be customized by extending or changing the existing code. In our case we did so by consulting the rule database for every method being edited. It is essential that the environment has full access to the rules.

- To support debugging of different languages, the debugger must be able to use an arbitrary source mapping between the custom language and the executable representation of the host environment. In our case we maintain this mapping from the source string through all transformation stages down to the bytecode. The debugger is fed with a custom function that maps source ranges to bytecode ranges. Since the debugger reuses the normal code editor of the programming environment, syntax highlighting works without additional support.

- Since all languages use the same underlying representation, there are no difficulties to share application state between different parts of the system. For example, a new language construct can access temporary variables, instance variables or globals. When a method is evaluated, it does not matter in which language it has been implemented. Block closures can be passed around, no matter what origin they have and from what language context they are evaluated.

We see the following main challenges to implement a system like Helvetia in an existing environment like Eclipse: (1) replace the default editor, compiler and debugger with customized ones, (2) connect these to a central rule database (this requires communication between different Java VMs), and (3) establish a fine-grained mapping between bytecode and source code (by default Java only supports a line based mapping).

3.3 Conclusion

In this chapter we have presented the key ideas behind Helvetia, an environment for defining embedded languages and for integrating them into a host language and its existing tools. We have shown how Helvetia introduces textual, syntactical and semantical macros [Gerrits and Gabriëls, 2005] through an extensible rewriting system into an existing programming language that has no built-in macro processor. We have demonstrated how a host environment can be changed by introducing a few extension points into the standard compiler pipeline and the host tools.

Reusing the traditional code representation of the host system has numerous advantages: We achieve a tight integration of different languages that work seamlessly with each other. We specify transformation rules using annotated methods, and specify the scope of these transformations using reflective facilities of the host language. Our approach works nicely with existing code and integrates well into the existing toolset. Fine-grained customizations such as syntax highlighting are readily supported.

Chapter 4

Helvetia Exemplified

> *"The only way to learn a new programming language is by writing programs in it."*
>
> — Dennis Ritchie

In this chapter we demonstrate various Helvetia language extensions. A prototype of Helvetia is implemented in Pharo Smalltalk [Black *et al.*, 2009], an open-source Smalltalk-80 [Goldberg and Robson, 1983] implementation. Details on how to download and get started with Helvetia can be found in Appendix A.

Readers unfamiliar with the syntax of Smalltalk might want to read the code examples in the remainder of this dissertation aloud and interpret them as normal sentences. An invocation to a method named `method:with:`, using two arguments looks like: `receiver method: arg1 with: arg2`. The semicolon separates messages that are sent to the same receiver. For example, `receiver method1: arg1; method2: arg2` sends the messages `method1:` and `method2:` to `receiver`. Other syntactic elements of Smalltalk are: the dot to separate statements: `statement1. statement2`; square brackets to denote code blocks or anonymous functions: `[ statements ]`; single quotes to delimit strings: `'a string'`; and double quotes delimit comments: `"comment"`. The caret `^` returns the result of the following expression.

This chapter starts in Section 4.1 with an introduction to parse-tree matching and code generation, two central concepts when developing language extensions with Helvetia. Then we dive into two examples of embedded languages that use the same underlying API of a graphical engine and transform it into a pidgin (Section 4.2) and a creole (Section 4.3) language. Finally, we describe the implementation of an argot for introducing transactional memory (Section 4.4). Other examples of Helvetia language extensions are listed in Appendix B.

4.1 Matching and Generating Code

The syntax for *tree pattern matching* and *quasiquoting* looks similar at first sight, however the two mechanisms serve entirely different purposes: While the tree pattern matching is used to identify and extract nodes from an existing parse-tree, the quasiquoting is used to construct and compose new parse-tree nodes. Both mechanisms are essential to the Helvetia rule system to conveniently specify transformation rules.

4.1.1 Tree Pattern Matching

Helvetia uses tree pattern matching [Kilpeläinen and Mannila, 1992] as the mechanism to identify specific parse-tree nodes in host language code. This infrastructure is based on the refactoring engine [Brant *et al.*, 1998] provided by the host language.

Tree patterns are specified using host language expressions that are annotated with optional meta-characters. The back-tick marks meta-nodes that are not required to match literally but that are variable. Table 4.1 gives an overview of the supported meta-characters following the initial back-tick.

Char	Type	Description
#	literal	Match a literal node like a number, boolean, character, string, or symbol.
.	statement	Match a statement in a sequence node.
@	list	When applied to a variable, match any expression. When applied to a statement, match a list of statements. When applied to a message, match a list of arguments.
`	recurse	When a match is found recurse into the matched node.

Table 4.1: Meta-characters of the tree pattern matching.

Listing 4.1 provides the source code of a simple method to illustrate the basic concepts of tree pattern matching. For example, the pattern `current isRoot` matches the single occurrence of the parse-tree node of `current isRoot`. The pattern `current `selector` matches all zero argument method invocation on the receiver `current`. In the example, these are `current isRoot` and `current parent`.

To match any method invocation on any object we can use the pattern ``@receiver `@selector: `@argument`. In our example the pattern matches `self resolve` and the loop with the message name `whileFalse:`. The inner parts of the loop are not

```
level
  | level current |
  level := 0.
  current := self resolve.
  [ current isRoot ] whileFalse: [
    level := level + 1.
    current := current parent ].
  ^ level
```

Listing 4.1: Example method to illustrate parse-tree matching.

matched, because by default the search does not recurse into already matched nodes. If we add a second back-tick to a meta-variable the search continues after a match recursively into the tree. For example, the modified query ``@receiver `@selector: ``@argument additionally matches current isRoot, level + 1 and current parent.

The pattern `#literal matches any literal node. In the example it matches the nodes of the numbers 0 and 1. The pattern `.statement matches a single statement. In the example, these are level := 0, current := self resolve, the complete loop, and ^ level. Again, the statements inside the loop are not matched, because by default the search does not recurse into already matched nodes.

The name of the meta-variables can be used to extract sub-parts of the parse-tree nodes after a successful match. If the same name is used multiple times, the parse-tree matcher uses unification. For example, the pattern `variable := `variable `@selector: `@argument matches level := level + 1 and current := current parent, but not current := self resolve because current and self are not the same.

4.1.2 Code Generation with Quasiquoting

To generate code from within Helvetia we use *quasiquoting*. The quasiquoting facilities in Helvetia are similar to ones known from languages like Lisp [Bawden, 1999]. Table 4.2 compares the quoting operators of various meta-programming systems. In Helvetia quasiquoting is a language extension implemented in Helvetia itself. Its syntax and semantics is summarized in the following list:

- A *quasiquoted* expression is prefixed with ``. It is delayed in execution and represents the AST of the enclosed expression at runtime.

	Scheme	MetaOCaml	Template Haskell	Helvetia
Quasiquote	`` `expr ``	`.<expr>.`	`[|expr|]`	`` ``expr ``
Unquote	`,expr`	`.~expr`	`$expr`	`` `,expr ``
Splice	`,@expr`	`.!expr`	`$expr`	`` `@expr ``

Table 4.2: Quoting operators for code generation.

- An *unquote* expression is prefixed with `` ` ``, and can be used within a quasiquoted expression. It is executed when the AST is built and can be used to combine smaller quasiquoted values to larger ones.

- A *splice* expression is prefixed with `` `@ ``. It is evaluated at compile-time and the result is spliced-into the code. If the returned expression is not an AST, it is automatically lifted to the AST level.

As an example we demonstrate how to generate code to calculate x^n, where n is a positive integer. The method below is a recursive definition of this method written in regular Smalltalk:

```
raise: x to: n
  ^ n = 1
    ifTrue: [ x ]
    ifFalse: [ (self raise: x to: n - 1) * x ]
```

If we want to avoid the recursion at runtime and instead generate code that directly calculates the result for a given integer n we annotate the code with quasiquote and unquote operators:

```
raise: aNode to: n
  ^ n = 1
    ifTrue: [ aNode ]
    ifFalse: [ ``(`,(self raise: aNode to: n - 1) * `,aNode) ]
```

When evaluating `self raise:` `` ``x `` `to:` 3 with a variable node `` ``x ``, a parse-tree is constructed that multiplies the variable x three times with itself yielding the AST x * x * x. Using the splice operator we can insert the generated parse-tree anywhere into the code. For example:

```
qubic: x
    ^ `@(self raise: x to: 3)
```

At compile-time this creates code equivalent to:

```
qubic: x
    ^ x * x * x
```

4.2 A Pidgin: Mondrian

Mondrian [Meyer *et al.*, 2006] is a graph based visualization framework that provides a declarative Smalltalk API for users to specify new visualizations and compose existing ones.

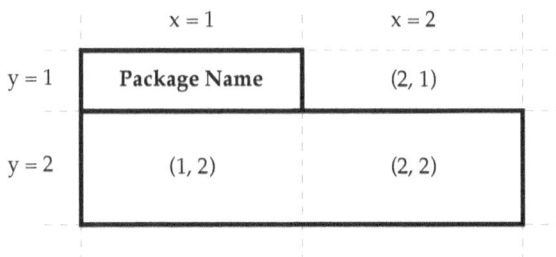

Figure 4.1: A UML package shape in Mondrian.

One of the features of Mondrian is an API to compose custom shapes out of basic ones, called FormsBuilder. The FormsBuilder is inspired by CSS 3 and uses a grid to align primitive graphical elements such as text labels and boxes. The code below in Listing 4.2 creates a UML package shape as depicted in Figure 4.1. The package shape is built from a 2 × 2 grid.

The first column and row are told to grow to enclose their children. The second column and row are told to fill the remaining space. In cell (1, 1) we place a bordered LabelShape. In cell (1, 2) we place a bordered RectangleShape that spans two horizontal cells.

Mondrian provides an internal DSL that offers a high-level interface for composing visualizations. While it makes the composition easy, there is still a considerable amount of syntactic noise that makes the script hard to read.

```
aBuilder row grow.                              " defines row sizing "
aBuilder row fill.

aBuilder column grow.                           " define column sizing "
aBuilder column fill.

aBuilder x: 1 y: 1 add: (LabelShape new         " define the cells "
   text: [ :each | each name ];
   borderColor: #black;
   borderWidth: 1;
   yourself).
aBuilder x: 1 y: 2 w: 2 h: 1 add: (RectangleShape new
   borderColor: #black;
   borderWidth: 1;
   width: 200;
   height: 100;
   yourself)
```

Listing 4.2: Traditional Mondrian Forms Builder API.

We incrementally bend the syntax of the host language towards a more suitable DSL, first by creating a pidgin, and then by creating a creole. Our final goal is to be able to define the visualizations using a simple syntax resembling cascading style-sheets (CSS), which offers a compact notation to programmers and designers to declaratively specify layout and design of web sites.

If we have a look at the code in Listing 4.2 we see that the noise is caused by certain semantic elements that are required to make this example run as Smalltalk code conforming to the original Mondrian API. We discover three things that are repetitive and that could be simplified:

1. The variable `aBuilder` is referenced in every rule as an entry point to construct and configure the different parts of the forms.

2. The specification of the cells and their content is repetitive and rather hard to read.

3. The instantiation of different shapes is cumbersome as in this case the host language syntax is rather verbose.

The code in Listing 4.3 addresses these issues.

```
row = grow.
row = fill.
column = grow.
column = fill.
(1 , 1) = label
          text: [ :each | each name ];
          borderColor: #black;
          borderWidth: 1.
(1 , 2) - (2 , 1) = rectangle
          borderColor: #black;
          borderWidth: 1;
          width: 200;
          height: 100.
```

Listing 4.3: Pidgin: Eliminating syntactic noise.

While the above code is syntactically valid and is parsed by the standard Smalltalk parser, it is not semantically valid. For example numbers do not implement the operator ',', and `column` is an unknown variable.

4.2.1 Specifying the Mondrian Pidgin

In our implementation, the above pidgin example is transformed transparently into the code from Listing 4.2. This kind of transformation simplifies the amount and complexity of source code significantly. The transformation is specified at the AST level using two transformation rules that are applied by the compiler after parsing.

The syntax of the Mondrian pidgin can be parsed by the traditional parser of the Smalltalk host language. However, we need to apply several transformations to get the semantics right. We define a set of transformation rules that are applied by Helvetia after parsing the code from Listing 4.3:

```
1  MondrianPidgin class>>rowColumnTransformation
2      <transform>
3      ^ TreeRule new
4          expression: 'row = `@expr';
5          expression: 'column = `@expr';
6          action: [ :ast |
7              ast swapWith: ``(`,(ast method arguments first)
```

```
8            `,(ast receiver)
9            `,(ast at: '`@expr')) ]


10  <MondrianPidgin class>>cellTransformation
11      <transform>
12      ^ TreeRule new
13        expression: '(`@x , `@y) = `@expr';
14        expression: '(`@x , `@y) - (`@w , `@h) = `@expr';
15        action: [ :ast |
16          ast swapWith: ``(`,(ast method arguments first)
17            x: `,(ast at: '`@x')
18            y: `,(ast at: '`@y')
19            w: `,(ast at: '`@w' ifAbsent: [ 1 ])
20            h: `,(ast at: '`@h' ifAbsent: [ 1 ])
21            add: ``(`,(Shapes at: (context at: '`var') name)
22                new `,(ast at: '`@expr'))) ]
```

The transformation rules are split into two methods. Each of these methods is tagged with the method annotation <transform> (lines 2 and 11), so that the compiler knows it has to apply these transformations before performing semantic analysis. Each rule consists of two match expressions (lines 4–5 and 13–14) to find particular parse-tree nodes. In our context these patterns match the specific constructs we introduced in Listing 4.3.

The action blocks (lines 6–9 and 15–22) perform a transformation on the matched AST node. For example, the first rules matches expressions of the form row = grow and transforms them into aBuilder row grow. The second transformation rule matches expressions of the form (1 , 2) = rectangle and transforms them into aBuilder x: 1 y: 2 add: LabelShape new. The expression `,(ast method arguments first) (lines 7 and 16) returns a reference to first argument aBuilder of the generated method.

The two methods are all that is needed to implement the Mondrian pidgin. The swapWith: method call replaces the matched AST node with the new code. Since all AST nodes carry information about their original source origin, a debugger is able to step through and properly highlight the recomposed code fragments. Newly generated code is marked as hidden, so that the user of the pidgin does not see it in the debugger. Language developers are given the possibility to inspect and debug generated code.

4.3 A Creole: Mondrian

The pidgin shows an improvement over the original Smalltalk code, but our goal is to obtain an even more concise CSS-like language as in listing Listing 4.4.

```
shape {
    cols: #grow, #fill;
    rows: #grow, #fill;
}
label {
    position: 1 , 1;
    text: [ :each | each name ];
    borderColor: #black;
    borderWidth: 1;
}
rectangle {
    position: 1 , 2;
    colspan: 2;
    borderColor: #black;
    borderWidth: 1;
    width: 200;
    height: 100;
}
```

Listing 4.4: Creole: A CSS-like syntax.

The code above does not follow Smalltalk syntax. At this point, the assumption of a pidgin relying on the host syntax starts to get in our way.

The solution is to allow the definition of a new parser that handles the creole syntax. We usually also want to integrate the new language constructs with the host language or with other language constructs. In our example, the code text: [:each | each name] provides such a case in which we parameterize the shape specification with a Smalltalk expression.

As shown in the following section, Helvetia offers a mechanism for writing a custom parser that can also include productions external to the language at hand. Like this we can accommodate any syntax.

4.3.1 Specifying the Mondrian Creole

In contrast to a pidgin, a creole requires a custom parser and Helvetia offers the possibility to define one. For example, for the creole we presented in Listing 4.4 we define the following grammar rules as individual methods of the class CSSParser:

```
CSSParser>>rules = { rule }
CSSParser>>rule = selector "{" declarations "}"
CSSParser>>selector = #identifier
CSSParser>>declarations = declaration { ";" declaration }
CSSParser>>declaration = #keywordMessage
```

This grammar definition looks very similar to the Extended Backus-Naur Form (EBNF) [Wirth, 1977]. In fact, it is a DSL for parser generators implemented in Helvetia. As an extension to EBNF we allow productions to reference grammar rules of other languages. The name of external grammar rules are prefixed with a hash character #. For example, the CSS selector is simply a Smalltalk identifier, and the declaration of a property is a keyword message (a Smalltalk method name with arguments, but without receiver) of the host language.

Next we create a new subclass of CSSParser called CSSTranslator, to reuse the abstract grammar definition and to augment it with productions to transform the parse-tree nodes to the host language AST [Bracha, 2007]. The operator '==>' attaches semantic actions to the grammar defined in the superclass. Again we use quasiquoting to build the AST of the host language. Two of CSSTranslator's parse-tree transformations look like in the following listing. The other grammar productions are similarly defined.

```
1  CSSTranslator>>rules
2    ^ super rules ==> [ :ast | ``(buildOn: aBuilder `,ast) ]


3  CSSTranslator>>rule
4    ^ super rule ==> [ :ast |
5      self
6        transform: (ast at: 'selector')
7        declarations: (ast at: 'declarations') ]
```

This assigns semantic actions to the productions defined in the superclass. The argument ast contains the parse nodes built by the grammar productions of the superclass. Line 2 uses quasiquoting to define the method header and to embed the AST nodes of the rules into its body. Line 5–7 call a helper method build:declarations:

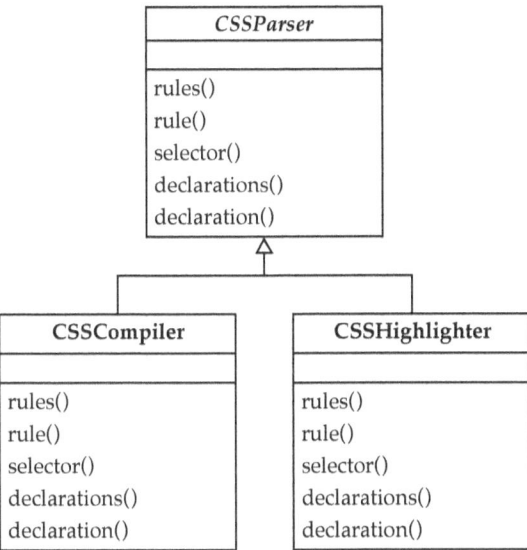

Figure 4.2: The CSS Parser Hierarchy.

with the selector token and a collection of declaration messages to build a Smalltalk AST.

To tell the system to use our custom parser instead of the default one, we use a method annotation <parse> on the classes where we want to use the custom syntax. The code in Listing 4.4 is parsed, transformed and eventually compiled to an executable representation identical to the methods we manually wrote in Listing 4.2 and Listing 4.3.

```
MondrianCreole class>>cssParser
    <parse>
    ^ CSSTranslator
```

One minor problem at this point is that the syntax highlighter in the code editor does not adapt to the custom syntax yet. As before, we create a new subclass of CSSParser named CSSHighlighter that underlines the selectors and dispatches to standard Smalltalk highlighting for the definitions. Again this is achieved by overriding the appropriate methods of CSSParser. For example, the selector method is defined in CSSHighlighter as follows. The arrow operator '->' associates a text format to a collection of tokens.

```
CSSHighlighter>>selector
    ^ super selector ==> [ :token | token -> TextEmphasis underlined ]
```

```
    <highlight>
```

```
MondrianCreole class>>cssHighlighter
    <highlight>
    ^ CSSHighlighter
```

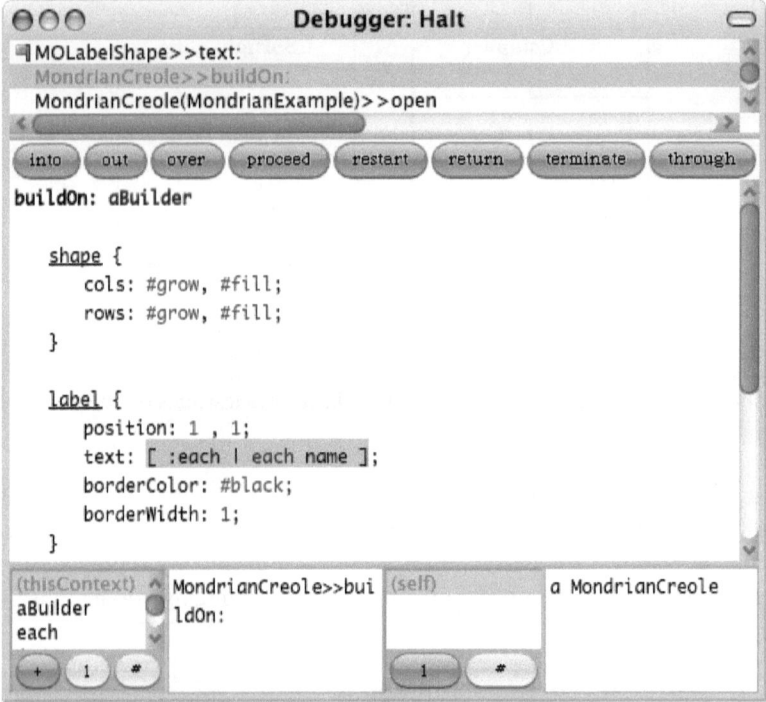

Figure 4.3:

LabelShape>>text:

The changes shown in this section are all that is needed to adapt the debugger too. Figure 4.3 shows a live result of stepping through the execution of the script building the UML package shape.

4.4 An Argot: Transactional Memory

Most dynamic programming languages have inherently weak support for concurrent programming and synchronization. While such languages relieve the programmer of the burden to allocate and free memory by using advanced garbage collection algorithms, they do not provide similar abstractions to ease concurrent programming [Grossman, 2007].

Software transactional memory (STM) [Herlihy, 1991; Herlihy and Moss, 1993] is an attractive mechanism for concurrency control. Introducing STM into an existing language provides a concrete use case for changing the execution semantics without changing the syntax of the language. A piece of library code that is used as part of transactional code should continue to work without requiring any adaptation. Unlike a pidgin, which bends the host syntax in ways that break the semantics, an argot more subtly reinterprets the semantics of otherwise valid code.

In this section we present in detail the implementation of transactional memory at the language level using Helvetia. We furthermore validate our approach in the context of the host language and compare it with related work.

4.4.1 Programming with transactions

Transactions offer an intuitively simple mechanism for synchronization of concurrent actions. They do not require users to declare specific locks or guard conditions that have to be fulfilled. Moreover transactions can be used without prior knowledge of the specific objects that might be modified. Transactions are global, yet multiple transactions can run in parallel. The commit protocol checks for conflicts and makes the changes visible to other processes atomically.

```
tree := BTree new.
lock := Semaphore forMutualExclusion.
lock critical: [ tree at: #a put: 1 ].                    " writing "
lock critical: [ tree at: #a ].                           " reading "
```

Listing 4.5: Lock-based access of a shared data structure.

```
tree := BTree new.
[ tree at: #a put: 1 ] atomic.                          " writing "
tree at: #a.                                            " reading "
```

Listing 4.6: Transactional access of a shared data structure.

In Listing 4.5 we see the traditional way of using a semaphore to ensure mutual exclusion on a tree data structure. The key problem is that *all* read and write accesses to the tree must be guarded using the same lock to guarantee safety. A thread-safe tree must be fully protected in all of its public methods. Furthermore, we cannot easily have a second, unprotected interface to the same tree for use in a single-threaded context.

In Listing 4.6 we present the code that is needed to safely access the collection using a transaction: the write access is put into a block that tells the Smalltalk environment to execute its body within a transaction. The read access can happen without further concurrency control. As long as all write accesses occur within the context of a transaction, read accesses are guaranteed to be safe. The optimistic commit protocol of the transaction guarantees safety by (i) ensuring that no write conflicts have occurred with respect to the previous saved state, and by (ii) atomically updating the global object state.

To make the code using transactions as simple as possible we provide two methods for running code as part of a transaction. These methods are extensions to the standard Smalltalk library and do not affect the language syntax or runtime.

- Sending `atomic` causes the receiving block closure to run as a new transaction. Upon termination of the block any changes are committed atomically. If a conflict is detected, all modifications are cancelled and a commit conflict exception is raised.

- Sending `atomicIfConflict:` causes the receiving block to run as a new transaction. Instead of raising an exception if a conflict occurs, the block argument is evaluated. This enables developers to take a specific action, such as retrying the transaction or exploring the conflicting changes.

Further convenience methods can easily be built out of these two methods, for example a method to retry a transaction up to fixed number of times, or only to enter a transaction if a certain condition holds.

4.4.2 Inside transactions

In a nutshell, our software transactional memory implementation works as follows. We compile every method in the system twice, once for the transactional and once for the non-transactional context. On the transactional code we apply two transformations: (1) all state access is reified to be dispatched through the transactional context, and (2) method names and method sends are prefixed with __atomic__. Furthermore, we use method annotations to disable or customize these transformations in certain places, such as when primitive code is called or in the transactional infrastructure itself. A transaction is started by assigning a transaction manager to a thread-local variable and by calling an __atomic__ method. At the end of a transaction the cached changes are atomically checked for conflicts and applied to the involved objects. The transaction boundaries are handled at the language level using the reflective facilities of the host language.

The complete set of Helvetia transformation rules is presented below:

```
1   Object class>>transformAtomic
2      <attribute>
3      ^ ConditionRule new
4        if: [ :context | context isTransactional ]
5        then: (TreeRule new
6          expression: '`@receiver `@msg: `@args' do: [ :ast |
7            ast swapWith: ``(`,(ast at: '`@receiver')
8              `,('__atomic__' , (ast at: '`@msg:'))
9              `,(ast at: '`@args')) ];
10         expression: '`var := `@expr' do: [ :ast |
11           ast swapWith: ``(self
12             atomicInstVarAt: `,(ast binding index)
13             put: `,(ast at: '`@expr')) ];
14         expression: '`var' do: [ :ast |
15           ast swapWith: ``(self
16             atomicInstVarAt: `,(ast binding index)) ])
```

The code uses the <attribute> method annotation (line 2) to tell the compiler that the rules are expected to run after the symbols have been resolved (attributed). Line 4 makes sure that the transformation is performed only when compiling code for the transactional context. Lines 5–16 implement the actual transformations, exemplified in Table 4.3.

All message sends are prepended with __atomic__ to ensure that the execution stays in the atomic context. All state accesses, such as instance variable reads and writes,

6–9	Transform Message Sends
	`self printString` → `self __atomic__printString`
10–13	Transform Instance Variable Write
	`value := 'Atomic'` → `self atomicInstVarAt: 2 put: 'Atomic'`
14–16	Transform Instance Variable Read
	`value` → `self atomicInstVarAt: 2`

Table 4.3: Different semantic transformations for transactional memory.

are transformed to message sends and dispatched through the transaction manager. This allows us to delay modifications to objects, so that the changes are only visible within the current transaction. The number 2 in the examples above refers to the index of the named instance variable `value`. This slot index is retrieved from the attributed AST.

To trigger the compilation of a transactional and a non-transactional version of every method we hook into the compiler again using the `<attribute>` annotation. We copy the compilation context and spawn a new compilation path for the transaction context.

```
Object class>>compileTransactional: aContext
   <attribute>
   aContext isTransactional ifFalse: [
      aContext copy
         beTransactional;
         perform ].
   ^ nil
```

The static compilation model with the duality between normal compiled methods and methods compiled for the transactional context is depicted in Figure 4.4. Transactional methods are methods marked as hidden and are not visible to the developer and development tools but to the VM only.

Without additional work the use of the debugger becomes viable, because the Helvetia transformations preserve location integrity. Single stepping through transactional code looks exactly the same as the regular code, even if the semantics are different and involve a non-primitive state lookup.

In our previous works on transactional memory [Renggli and Nierstrasz, 2007] it was not possible to transparently step through transactional code, as the tools would display the generated code. The new implementation takes advantage of Helvetia:

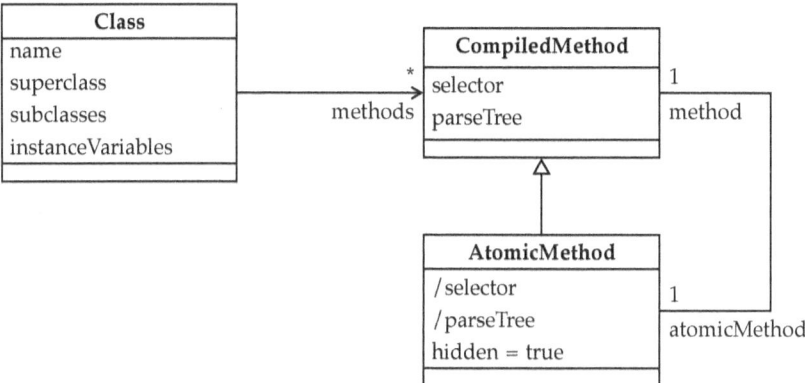

Figure 4.4: Static compilation model for transactional memory.

the implementation became significantly simpler and the tools continue to work as expected.

4.5 Conclusion

In this chapter we have presented the Helvetia rule system in practice. We have shown how the infrastructure for parse-tree matching and code generation provides an extensible macro system that supports the creation of pidgin, creole and argot languages.

Furthermore, we have exemplified the creation of language extension with Helvetia using three real-world language extensions. We have demonstrated how these language extensions blend into the existing tools and how we can mix embedded languages with the host language. Also, we have shown that a common code and data abstraction avoids an unnecessary interpretation layer and enables to transparently pass values between different languages without an explicit conversion.

Chapter 5

Combining Language Extensions

> *"Nothing of me is original. I am the combined effort of everybody I've ever known."*
>
> — Chuck Palahniuk

In this chapter we present *Language Boxes* and how to apply the concepts to embedded languages. Language boxes extend on the rule system of Helvetia and provide a modular and composable high-level model of tightly intermixed language extensions.

Language boxes are built on top of Helvetia and are used to describe and implement language features in a modular way. Our model works on an executable grammar model [Bracha, 2007] of the host language. A *language change* is used to specify a composition of this grammar together with the grammar of a different language. *Language concerns* denote a transformation from parse tokens to the abstract syntax tree (AST) nodes of the host language. Other concerns are supported to specify additional behavior of the tools, such as syntax highlighting, contextual menus, error correction or autocompletion. The *language scope* describes the contexts in which the new language features are enabled. Language boxes yield a high-level model to cleanly embed language extensions and language changes into an existing host environment.

This chapter is structured as follows: In Section 5.1 we present a introductory example. In Section 5.2 we introduce the model of Language Boxes. Section 5.3 gives an overview of the implementation identifying the general principles and techniques necessary to build the proposed system. Section 5.4 shows the implementation in action. Section 5.5 evaluates and summarizes our approach to introduce new features to an existing language.

5.1 Language Boxes in Practice

The Smalltalk programming language does not include a literal type for regular expressions. Traditionally regular expressions are instantiated by passing a string to a constructor method of the class Regexp. To match a sequence of digits one would, for example, write: Regexp on: '\d+'. For developers such lengthy code is repetitive to write. Furthermore, the code is inefficient as the regular expression is parsed and built at runtime. In this section we propose a language extension that adds regular expression literals to the language. This makes a good illustration for our framework, because regular expressions represent an already existing non-trivial domain-specific language that is currently not well integrated into the host system.

A new language box is created by subclassing LanguageBox. We use ordinary methods to define the characteristics of the language extension. In our example we start by creating a new language box called RegexpLanguageBox. We add the method change: returning a change object that determines how to transform the host language grammar.

```
RegexpLanguageBox>>change: aGrammar
    ^ LanguageChange new
        after: aGrammar literal;
        choice: '/' , '/' not star , '/'
```

The returned change specifies that the grammar fragment '/' , '/' not star , '/' is appended as an additional choice after the existing grammar production for literals. aGrammar literal returns the original production used to parse literal values in the host language.

The grammar extension is defined using a DSL for parser combinators, where the comma is used as a sequence operator and strings denote parsers for themselves. '/' not star is a parser that accepts zero or more occurrences of characters other than the slash. In this example the parser accepts any sequence of characters that start and end with the slash delimiter.

The editors, compiler and debugger will automatically pick up the language box and use its change definition to transform the grammar of the host language. Anywhere in the source code where a literal is expected a regular expression with the specified syntax is accepted as well. At this point, the language box does not yet specify any additional behavior for the tools.

```
RegexpLanguageBox>>compile: aToken
    ^ (Regexp on: aToken string) lift: aToken
```

The above method is a hook method that is automatically called by the compiler to transform the parse-tree tokens of the language extension to the host language AST. In our example we instantiate a regular expression object from the token value. The method `lift:` converts a host language value into an AST node. In this case it takes the regular expression object and wraps it into a literal node. The original token is passed into the literal node to retain the source mapping for the debugger.

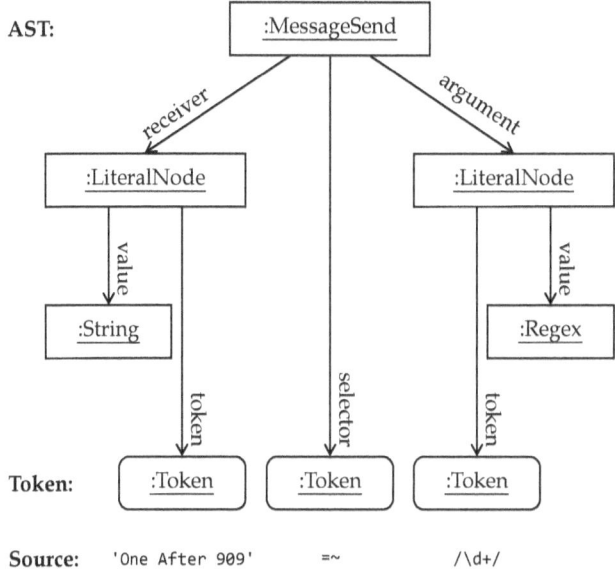

Figure 5.1: From the source code to the AST of the host language.

Expressions with literal regular expressions can now be used anywhere in the source code, for example `'One After 909' =~ /\d+/`. As depicted in Figure 5.1 the transformed grammar of the host language parses the source code and uses our function `compile:` to transform the input to the host AST. Note that '`=~`' is a matching operator for regular expressions. This operator is not a language extension, but a method implemented in the `String` class. In this example, the matched sub-string `'909'` is returned.

The syntax highlighter in the editor recognizes the regular expression syntax as valid, but it still colors the source using the default font style. To change this, we add a syntax highlighting concern to the language box:

```
RegexpLanguageBox>>highlight: aToken
    ^ aToken -> Color orange
```

With only a few lines of code we have demonstrated how to extend the syntax of a general-purpose language with a new literal type, how to define the transformation to the host language AST and how to integrate it into editors by customizing the syntax highlighting.

5.2 Language Box Model

Parser, compiler and associated development tools are usually black boxes. Extending, changing or replacing the default behavior is not easy and thus discouraged. We propose a high-level language model that provides us with fine grained access to the different syntactic elements of the host language without revealing too much of the underlying implementation. Furthermore we provide a set of extension points for the language grammar to allow developers to extend the compiler and available development tools. Language extensions should be open, in the sense that they tightly integrate anywhere in the host language grammar without requiring special syntactical constructs to change between different language extensions.

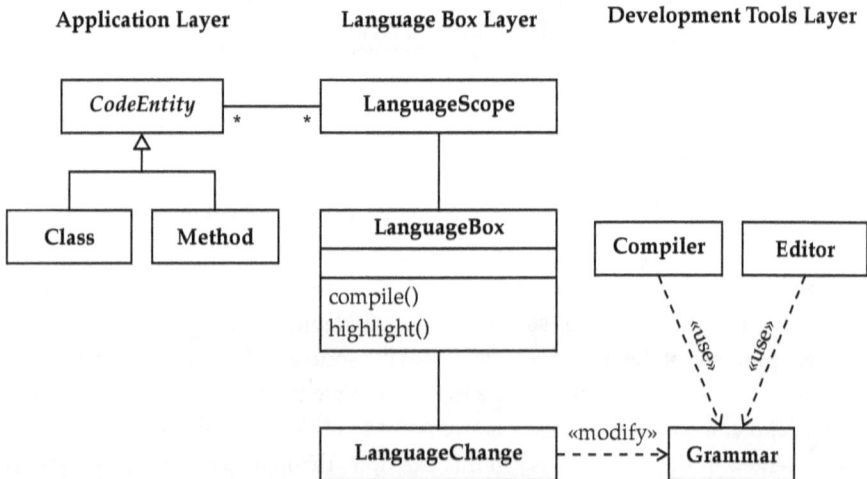

Figure 5.2: The interplay of the language box model with the application layer and the development tools.

As depicted in Figure 5.2 the language box model consists of three parts: In Section 5.2.1 we introduce the *language change*, which defines how the grammar of the host language is changed. Then in Section 5.2.2 we explain how *language concerns* customize the behavior of language extensions by attaching handlers to the grammar, such as for customized syntax highlighting, code completion, code expansion, error handling, refactoring, navigation, search or contextual menus. Finally in Section 5.2.3 we discuss the *language scope*, which is used to restrict the effect of a language box to certain parts of the application code.

5.2.1 Language Change

The language change is used to encapsulate a local grammar adaption [Lämmel, 2001] applied to the grammar of the host language. In our case the language extension is defined using a grammar fragment and a specification of how this fragment is composed with the grammar of the host language.

In Section 5.1 we added a new regular expression literal as an additional choice to the existing literals. This means the host language grammar rule was changed from

```
Literal ::= String / Number / Boolean
```

to

```
Literal ::= String / Number / Boolean / Regexp
```

where `Regexp` was defined as `Regexp ::= '/' , '/' not star , '/'`. In addition to appending to the end of a choice we also support various other composition strategies to combine the grammar of the host language and the new grammar fragment. These composition strategies are listed in Table 5.1.

Action	Composition	Production
replace	–	$R ::= X$
before	sequence	$R ::= X\,A$
after	sequence	$R ::= A\,X$
before	choice	$R ::= X\,/\,A$
after	choice	$R ::= A\,/\,X$

Table 5.1: Composition strategies for a grammar rule $R ::= A$. A is a symbol of the original grammar. X is the extending grammar fragment as defined by the language change. $X\,A$ denotes the sequence of X and A, $X\,/\,A$ denotes an ordered choice between X and A.

An important property of the language change is that the grammar composed into the host language might reference other productions from the existing grammar. This allows language designers to reuse existing features of the host language and closely integrate existing syntax with the language extension. Depending on the host language production we can decide to change the language box to replace the complete host language with a new grammar (for example when the start production of the grammar is replaced), or just to change individual features (for example when adding a new literal type).

While the inserted grammar fragment in our initial example was intentionally chosen to be trivial, it is possible to compose arbitrary complex grammars using the given composition strategies. Furthermore multiple composition strategies can be defined in the same language box, as we will demonstrate in Section 5.4 where Smalltalk and SQL are combined.

5.2.2 Language Concern

When changing or adding new language features, there are different concerns to integrate into the toolset of the application developers. First and foremost we need to specify a transformation from our language extension to the code representation of the host language. Optionally we might want to closely integrate the language extensions into the existing programming tools, such as editors and debuggers. This is done by adding concerns to the language box such as:

- **Compilation.** This concern describes the transformation from the AST nodes and parse-tree tokens of the language extension to the AST of the host language. We call this process *compilation* because it makes the language extension executable. Subsequently the host language AST is passed into the standard compiler tool-chain that compiles it further down into an efficiently executable representation.

- **Highlighting.** The syntax highlighter concern annotates the source ranges with color and font information, so that the editor and debugger are able to display properly colored and formatted text. The resulting source ranges and styling information is then passed into the standard editors for display.

- **Actions.** This concern provides a list of labels and associated actions that are integrated into the standard contextual menu of editors. This allows for context sensitive functionality, such as language specific refactorings. Thus unsuitable actions from the host language or other language extensions are not displayed when the user works in the context of a language extension.

Other concerns can be specified similarly, for example enhanced navigation and search facilities, error correction, code expansion templates, code completion, code folding, or pretty printing.

Concerns are implemented by overriding a default implementation. This facilitates the evolution of new language features, starting from a minimal language box that defines a change to the host grammar only. At a later point the language designer can incrementally add new concerns to make the language integrate more appropriately with the tools. In the introductory example we saw that the compilation and highlighting concerns were not specified in the beginning. In this case a default implementation caused the compiler to insert a null node and the highlighter to use the default text color.

5.2.3 Language Scope

To scope the effect of Language Boxes to well-defined fragments of the application source code, we need a way to specify the extent of the language changes within the application code. The scope identifies Language Boxes and the associated code entities, as depicted in Figure 5.2. Language developers can define a default scope. From coarse to fine grained the following scopes are supported:

- **System.** The system scope affects all the source code of the system without restriction. This is the default, if no more restrictive scope is specified.

- **Package.** The package scope affects all source artifacts contained in a particular package.

- **Class.** The class scope affects all source artifacts of a particular class, or its class hierarchy.

- **Method.** The method scope affects a particular method, or methods with a particular name.

Furthermore, we give the language box users the possibility to explicitly add a language box to a particular code entity (package, class, method) or to remove it. This effectively overrides the default scope and facilitates a fine-grained control of language features from within the application code. Language boxes are added or removed using either a context menu in the user interface or a declarative specification in the source code.

Whenever a tool requests a grammar at a specific location in the source code, the language box system determines all active Language Boxes by comparing their scope with the current source location. It then transforms the host language grammar according to the change specification in the Language Boxes and inserts the concerns for the active tool. This enables one to scope Language Boxes and their grammar changes to well-defined parts of the system.

5.3 Implementation

To validate the language box model, we have implemented it in Pharo [Black *et al.*, 2009], an open-source Smalltalk [Goldberg and Robson, 1983] platform. Language boxes are implemented on top of the Helvetia framework presented in Chapter 3. Helvetia provides the necessary hooks for Language Boxes that would otherwise need to be established separately:

Modular compiler. The internals of the compiler must be accessible so that a custom parser and an additional transformation phase can be introduced.

Extensible tools. The development environment and its tools must be extensible and have full access to structural and behavioral reflection.

Furthermore Language Boxes depend on the following host language features:

Structural reflection. The system must provide the capability to query packages, classes, and methods to determine when and where to apply Language Boxes.

Behavioral reflection. The AST must be a first class abstraction that can be queried, extended with new node types, built and transformed during compilation.

Our implementation of Language Boxes is lightweight because we reused as much functionality from the host environment as possible and we reuse all the hooks of the Helvetia system. Our approach is entirely implemented in Smalltalk. We do not change the underlying virtual machine. The implementation presented in this chapter consists of 640 lines of Smalltalk code, of which 410 lines consist of a reimplementation of the traditional Smalltalk parser as an executable grammar.

To facilitate transformations on the host language grammar we replaced the standard LALR parser with a *dynamic grammar*, a first-class representation of the parser that we can transform and recompose easily. We combine four different parser methodologies: scannerless parsers [Visser, 1997], parser combinators [Hutton and Meijer, 1996], parsing expression grammars [Ford, 2004] and packrat parsers [Ford, 2002]. We provide further details on the specification and implementation of grammars in Chapter 6.

Before a method is compiled, a custom parser for that particular compilation context is composed as depicted in Figure 5.3. This new parser is built by starting from the standard grammar of the host language and by applying the change objects of the active Language Boxes in the defined order.

Figure 5.4 depicts a fragment of the original Smalltalk grammar and the regular expression language extension that we introduced in Section 5.1. The composition algorithm takes the original grammar of the host language aGrammar and the grammar

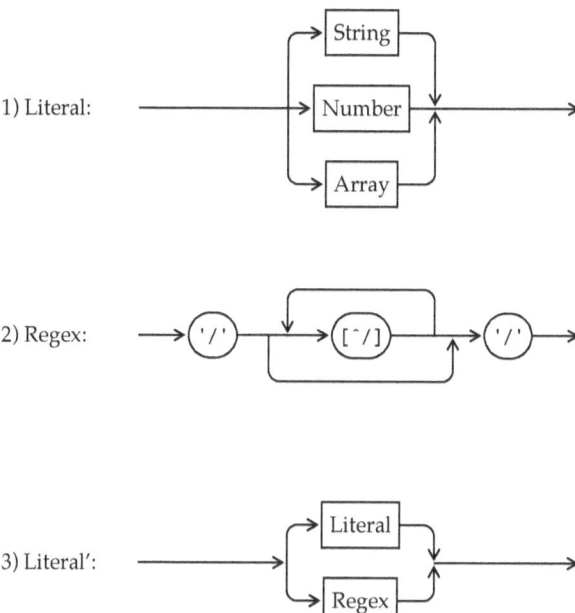

1) Literal:

2) Regex:

3) Literal':

Figure 5.3: The grammar composition visualized: (1) The slightly simplified production for literal values in Smalltalk, (2) the grammar fragment for regular expressions in the language box, and (3) the new production for literal values when the language box is active.

of the language extension `fragment` and composes them using the following algorithm. For conciseness we present the complete algorithm as a single method with nested conditional statements instead of the original implementation, which makes use of the strategy design pattern.

```
1   LanguageChange>>modify: aGrammar with: aLanguageBox
2       | wrapped replacement |
3       wrapped := fragment ==> [ :nodes |              " Figure 5.4(a) "
4           aLanguageBox
5               perform: aGrammar concern
6               with: (self transform: nodes) ].
7       replacement := action = 'replace'               " Figure 5.4(b) "
8           ifTrue: [ wrapped ]
9           ifFalse: [
10              action = 'before'
11                  ifTrue: [ composition with: wrapped with: production ]
12                  ifFalse: [
13                      action = 'after'
```

Traditional Smalltalk Grammar   Regular Expression Language Box

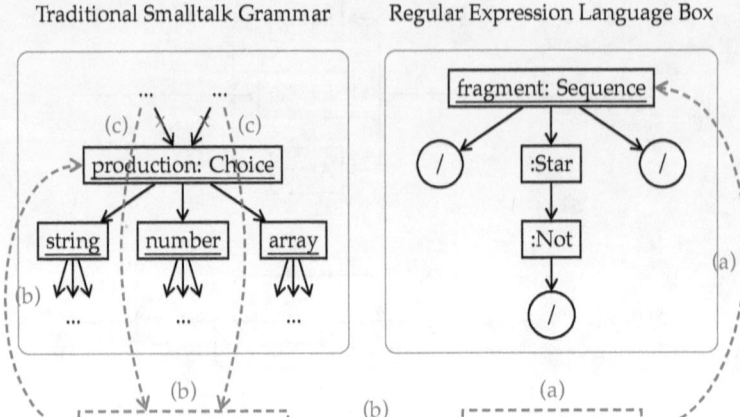

Figure 5.4: Traditional Smalltalk (left) and the regular expression extension (right) are combined in three steps to a single grammar: (a) the grammar fragment is wrapped with the action, (b) the wrapped fragment is combined with the existing grammar, and (c) all references to the original production are replaced with the combined one.

```
14          ifTrue: [ composition with: production with: wrapped ]
15          ifFalse: [ self error: 'Invalid composition.' ] ] ].
16   aGrammar replace: production with: replacement          " Figure 5.4(c) "
```

The composition algorithm modify:with: is implemented in the language change object. As input parameter the method takes the original language grammar aGrammar and the language box aLanguageBox responsible for this change. The actual transformation is a three step process:

1. Lines 3–6 fetch the grammar fragment and wrap it with the concern of the language box. This is achieved with the ==> operator which adds an action to a production. In our example the fragment is the new parser '/' , '/' not star , '/'. The concern depends on what the grammar is used for. If the grammar is used for compilation, the compile concern compile: is called; if the grammar is used for syntax highlighting, the highlight concern highlight: is called, *etc.* This does not change the structure of the resulting language grammar, but allows the production actions to produce different results for the different concerns. While the compilation concern requires a complete and valid AST the highlighting concern produces a stream of tokens with source position and color information.

2. Depending on the action and the selected composition a new grammar fragment is built (Figure 5.4(b)):

   a) The *replace action* (line 8) replaces the selected grammar production with the wrapped fragment.

   b) The *before action* (line 11) composes the wrapped fragment with the old production using either choice or sequence as composition operator.

   c) The *after action* (line 14) composes the old production with the wrapped fragment using either choice or sequence as composition operator.

   In our example the replacement production is defined as a choice that is added after the original literal production, *i.e.,* replacement ::= production / wrapped where production is the grammar fragment for literals in the original Smalltalk grammar.

3. Last on line 16 (Figure 5.4(c)) the grammar is told to replace all references to the original production with the replacement. This is done by traversing the complete grammar and replacing all the references to the old production with the new one. In our example all references to original literal production are replaced with the newly composed grammar fragment. This step ensures that the new grammar can parse regular expressions everywhere the host syntax would expect a literal.

In Smalltalk, the unit of editing and compilation is the method. This facilitates our language box model and enables a straightforward integration with the editor and other tools. The small and well-defined unit of editing eases the way for Language Boxes, however it is not a strict requirement. Depending on the granularity of the language scopes to be supported, grammar changes could be applied at the level of packages, files, classes or methods. The scoping of Language Boxes depends on the reflective capabilities of the host system [Foote and Johnson, 1989].

5.4 Case Study

To demonstrate the applicability of Language Boxes in practice, we present and discuss a more elaborate language extension. The goal is to embed a subset of the *Structured Query Language* (SQL) in the host language. Furthermore SQL should be extended so that values within the query can be safely replaced with expressions from the host language.

The following method shows a typical example of an embedded SQL query:

```
SQLQueries>>findUser: aString
  | query rows |
  query := 'SELECT * FROM users WHERE username = "' ,
    aString asEscapedSql , '"'.
  rows := SQLSession execute: query.
  ^ rows first
```

The query is concatenated from a series of strings and the input parameter aString. The composition of SQL from strings is not only error prone and cumbersome, but also introduces possible security exploits. The developer has to pay attention to correctly escape all input, otherwise an attacker might be able to manipulate the original SQL statement.

The following method shows the improved version using a language box for SQL statements:

```
SQLQueries>>findUser: aString
  | rows |
  rows := SELECT * FROM users
          WHERE username = @(aString).
  ^ rows first
```

SQL statements can be used anywhere in the host language where an expression is expected. The syntax of the SQL expression is automatically verified when compiling the code, assembled and executed, and the result is passed back into the host language as a collection of row objects. SQL itself is extended with a special construct @(...) to embed host language values into the query.

5.4.1 Adding an SQL Language Extension

Since SQL is a language on its own and considerably more complex than the regular expression language we saw before, we use an external class to define its grammar. To do this, we took advantage of the same infrastructure that we used to define a mutable model of the host language grammar. We implemented the syntax specification described for SQLite[1] which is almost identical to SQL92, but leaves out some of the more obscure features.

To combine the host language and SQL, we create a new language box called SQLLanguageBox. Again we specify a change method that describes how the new language is integrated into the host language:

---

1 http://www.sqlite.org/syntaxdiagrams.html

```
1  SQLanguageBox>>change: aSmalltalkGrammar
2      | sqliteGrammar compositeChange |
3      sqliteGrammar := SQLiteGrammar new.
4      compositeChange :=
5          (LanguageChange new
6              before: aSmalltalkGrammar expression;
7              choice: sqliteGrammar)
8        + (LanguageChange new
9              before: sqliteGrammar literalValue;
10             choice: '@(' , aSmalltalkGrammar expression , ')').
11     ^ compositeChange
```

On line 3 we instantiate the SQL grammar defined in the class SQLiteGrammar. In this example a single grammar transformation is not enough. On lines 5–7 we extend the production for host language expressions with SQL as an additional choice that is added before the original expression production. On lines 8–10 we extend the production for SQL literal values with a new syntax that lets Smalltalk expressions be part of SQL. The two changes are composed using the + operator and returned on line 11.

Note that the first change object introduces ambiguity into the host language grammar. Intentionally we decide that the SQL grammar should take precedence over the Smalltalk expression production and insert the SQL grammar before the expression production of the host language. SELECT * FROM users is both a syntactically valid SQL statement and a syntactically valid Smalltalk expression[2]. Since we added the SQL grammar to the beginning of the original host language production any expression is first tried with the SQL grammar. If this does not work, the original production of the host language expression will take over.

The problem that an SQL expression can potentially hide valid Smalltalk code remains open. The current implementation gives the responsibility to detect and avoid such problems to the language developer. Language boxes provide the tools to tightly control the scope of language changes, as discussed in Section 5.2.3. Furthermore, conflicting language changes can always be surrounded by special tokens to make the intention absolutely clear. This can be seen in the example above on line 10 where Smalltalk expressions in SQL are surrounded by @(...). If possible we try to avoid such extra tokens as they clutter the close integration of the new language. When integrating SQL into Smalltalk this is less of a problem, as SQL is a very strict language with a rigid and very verbose syntax. A test run based on a large collection

---

2 In Smalltalk, this would send the message users to the variable FROM, and then multiply the result with the variable SELECT.

of open-source Smalltalk code with a total of over 1 200 000 expression statements revealed that none of them parsed as valid SQL.

Similar to the regular expression example we define a compilation concern that tells the language box how to compile the new expression to the host language. In this example we do not receive a single token, but the complete AST as it is produced by the SQL grammar.

```
1  SQLLanguageBox>>compile: anSQLNode
2     | nodes query |
3     nodes := anSQLNode allLeaves collect: [ :token |
4        token isToken
5           ifTrue: [ token string lift: token ]
6           ifFalse: [ ``(`,token asEscapedSql) ] ].
7     query := nodes fold: [ :a :b | ``(`,a , ' ' , `,b) ].
8     ^ ``(SQLSession execute: `,query)
```

The compilation concern flattens all the leaf nodes of the SQL AST (line 3) and transforms the input to host language AST nodes (lines 4–6). Tokens of the SQL AST are transformed to literal nodes in the host language (line 5). If the node comes from embedded Smalltalk code, we automatically wrap the expression with a call to asEscapedSql to ensure it is properly escaped (line 6). Finally we concatenate all the nodes to a single query expression (line 7), which is then sent to the current SQL session manager (line 8). Again, we use the quasiquoting facilities provided by Helvetia to generate and compose code fragments of the host language, see Section 4.1 for details.

5.4.2 Restricting the Scope of a Language Extension

As we noted in our introductory example, by default a language box is active in the complete system. In many cases this is not desired, especially when a language change is more intrusive. We provide two different ways of modeling the scope of a language extension. While the first one is aimed at language designers, the second one targets language users who want to select and activate available language extensions while working in their code.

The *language designer* can specify a scope for a language by overriding the scope method in the language box. The default implementation of the method returns a system scope, but frameworks might want to reduce the scope to certain class hierarchies, packages, classes or methods. This feature makes use of the reflective facilities of the host language to determine if a given language box is active in a specific compilation context.

The *language user* can further change the scope of a language box through the code editor. As an extension we added menu commands that allow developers to add and remove language extensions from code entities like packages, classes and methods. This is useful for language extensions that make sense in different smaller scopes which cannot be foreseen by the language designer. Furthermore we extended the code editor with functionality to display the active extensions, so that the developer knows what he is expected to write. Also distinct syntax highlighting (*i.e.*, different background colors) in the language definition can help developers to know in which context they are currently working.

5.4.3 Mixing Different Language Extensions

The SQL language extension blends nicely with the host language, as well as the regular expression language extension we presented previously. For example we can use both language extensions at the same time, together with the host language:

```
rows := SELECT * FROM users
        WHERE username = @(aString ~= /\s*(\w+)\s*/)
```

This example transparently expands to the following (more verbose) code:

```
rows := SQLSession execute: 'SELECT * FROM users WHERE username = ' ,
    (aString ~= (Regexp on: '\s*(\w+)\s*')) asEscapedSql
```

The compiler automatically ensures that the SQL statement is syntactically valid, that all values injected into the statement are properly escaped and that the query is automatically executed within the current session.

5.4.4 Tool Integration

Adding syntax highlighting to the SQL expressions is straightforward. Contrary to the regular expression that was highlighted using a single color, the SQL extension is more complex and we have to deal with many different kinds of keywords, operators and expression types. To avoid having to specify the highlighting for every production within the language box itself, we allow language developers to specify an external class that specifies the concern-specific production actions. In the case of syntax highlighting these actions return the color and font information.

```
SQLLanguageBox>>highlight
   ^ SQLiteHighlighter
```

Adding a context menu item that links to the SQL documentation is a matter of adding the method:

```
SQLLanguageBox>>menu: aMenu using: anSQLNode
    ^ aMenu
        addMenuItem: 'SQLite Documentation'
        action: [ WebBrowser open: anSQLNode documentationUrl ]
```

Clicking on the menu item opens a web browser on the URL returned by the AST node under the cursor. The method `documentationUrl` is implemented to dispatch to the parent node, if no documentation is available at the most specific AST node.

Figure 5.5 depicts a standard Smalltalk code browser and a debugger on the presented example. The upper parts of both windows show the navigation context, which in the code browser is the currently edited package, class and method; in the debugger this is the execution stack. In both cases the lower part shows the source code of the method properly highlighted.

The transformations as defined by the compilation concern are not visible to end-users that work at the level of source-code. The transformations are only visible at the level of the compiled bytecode. All tools, including the debugger, display the original source code only. Stepping through custom languages in the debugger works similarly to traditional Smalltalk. Since all our transformations are on the level of the standard AST nodes and tokens, their original location in the source code can be traced back. The use of the AST to highlight the current execution position is a standard feature of the debugger. Generated nodes that do not have a physical position in the source code are skipped over when stepping through with the debugger.

Another example of how tightly Language Boxes integrate into the host language are breakpoints. In traditional Smalltalk breakpoints are implemented by invoking the method `halt` at the desired position in the source code. This method is implemented by the system. It stops the execution of the active process and opens a debugger at the current execution point. Since breakpoints are implemented at the level of AST nodes, they continue to work even within language extensions. Upon execution of a `halt` instruction the debugger opens up and automatically highlights the currently active code statement.

5.5 Conclusion

In this chapter we have presented Language Boxes, a novel model to change syntax and semantics of the host language. We have presented the concepts, an imple-

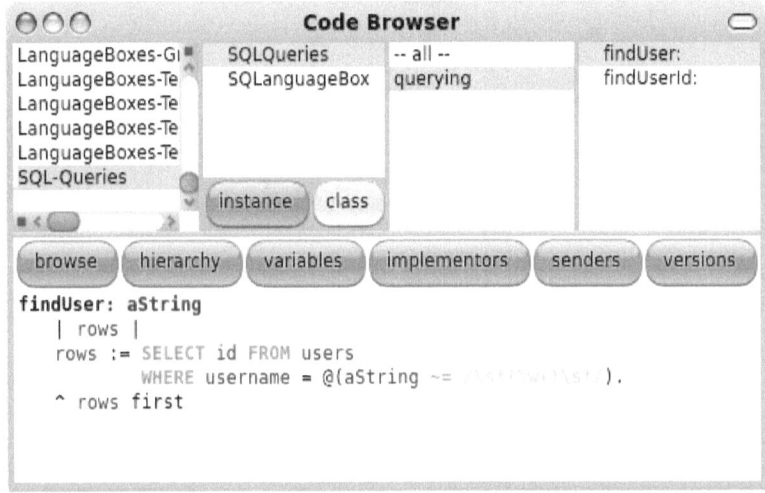

(a)

(b)

Figure 5.5:

mentation and two examples of Language Boxes. We have demonstrated how Language Boxes encapsulate language extensions and enable mixing different language changes. Finally, we have pointed out how existing tools are closely integrated with new language features.

The solution proposed in this chapter has the following properties:

Model. The language box model encapsulates changes to the grammar of the host language and defines different concerns that specify the behavior of the language extension in the tools. The scope defines the context in the source code where the language extension is active.

Modular. Language boxes are modular. Language extensions can be independently developed and deployed. The use of parser combinators makes it possible to combine grammars and even to support ambiguous ones in a meaningful way.

Concerns. Tools can be extended with language specific concerns. Language extensions can be developed incrementally. While the compilation concern is usually defined first, editor integration can be provided later.

Homogeneous Language Integration. Language boxes use the abstract code representation of the host language, different languages can be arbitrarily composed, access the same data and pass control to each other.

Homogeneous Tool Integration. The IDE, and especially the debugging tools, continue to work and actively support the language extensions. Stepping through a mixture of code from different languages poses no problem either. Changing and recompiling the source code on the fly from within the debugger is viable, this being an inherited feature from the host language.

Language boxes provide a model to extend the host language and as such are well suited to define embedded DSLs [Hudak, 1996]. Language boxes are implemented in the host language and are thus an internal domain-specific language themselves. This makes our approach adaptable to new requirements, as well as enabling a close integration with the host language.

The language box compiler is twice as slow as the modified Helvetia compiler, because a custom parser has to be composed for every compilation context. The parsing itself is not noticeably slower than with the LALR parser and there is no visible lag even for syntax highlighting, as methods tend to be short and memoizing packrat parsers guarantee linear time. To improve the speed of batch compilation — for example when loading an external package — we plan to add grammar caches in a further release.

Different Language Boxes can potentially influence or conflict with each other and the host language. We could rarely observe this problem in practice though, since most language changes are clearly scoped and often affect different parts of the original grammar. Two Language Boxes that add new literal types could result in a potentially ambiguous grammar where one language extension hides another one. In this case, the language extension that was loaded last will take precedence over the language extension loaded earlier. This could introduce unexpected side-effect into the code of the user. In Section 6.2.3 we present a way of detecting and notifying the user about such problems.

Chapter 6

Dynamic Grammars

> *"Within a computer natural language is unnatural."*
>
> — Alan Perlis

Grammars for programming languages are traditionally specified statically. They are hard to compose and reuse due to ambiguities that inevitably arise. In this chapter we present the *PetitParser* framework that combines ideas from scannerless parsing, parser combinators, parsing expression grammars and packrat parsers to model grammars and parsers as objects that can be reconfigured dynamically. Being able to cheaply transform and recompose grammars is a requirement for Language Boxes as presented in Chapter 5.

It is common practice to define formal grammars using a dedicated specification language which is then transformed into executable form by code generation. Typically these transformation algorithms validate that the grammar is a subset of *Context Free Grammars* (CFGs), such as LL(k), LR(k), or LALR(k). Then the algorithm optimizes and transforms the grammar into a parser. While this process can give parse-time guarantees and ensure that the parse is unambiguous, the resulting parsers are inherently static. The grammar is hard-coded and cannot be easily changed (at runtime) nor can it be easily composed with other grammars. Numerous researchers have tried to address these issues in the past [Schwerdfeger and Wyk, 2010; Bravenboer and Visser, 2009]. Earley and SGLR(k) parsers are composable [Earley, 1970; Bravenboer, 1997; Visser, 1997], however the parse results are usually ambiguous and the grammar definition is static and cannot be changed after compilation.

Language Boxes require a grammar model that is capable of parsing arbitrary programming languages. Furthermore, Language Boxes need to reflect on the language grammars and have the possibility to cheaply transform and recompose different grammars without any limitations on composability and ambiguity resolution. Our solution takes four existing parser methodologies and combines the best properties of each:

- *Scannerless Parsers* [Visser, 1997] combine lexical and context-free syntax into one grammar. This avoids the common problem of overlapping token sets when grammars are composed.

- *Parser Combinators* [Hutton, 1992; Hutton and Meijer, 1996] are building blocks for parsers modeled as a graph of composable objects; they are modular and maintainable, and can be changed, recomposed and reflected upon.

- *Parsing Expression Grammars* (PEGs) [Ford, 2004] provide ordered choice. Unlike CFGs, the ordered choice of PEGs always follows the first matching alternative and ignores other alternatives. PEGs are closed under union, intersection and complement, and they can recognize non-context free languages.

- *Packrat Parsers* [Ford, 2002] give linear parse time guarantees and avoid problems with left-recursion in PEGs through memoization [Warth *et al.*, 2008]. For efficiency reasons we do not memoize each rule, but only selected ones [Becket and Somogyi, 2008].

The remainder of this chapter is structured as follows: Section 6.1 introduces the PetitParser framework, a grammar infrastructure that makes it easy to dynamically reuse, compose, transform and extend grammars. Section 6.2 discusses important aspects of a dynamic approach, such as composition, correctness, tool support, and performance. Section 6.3 presents an overview of the related work, and Section 6.4 concludes this chapter.

6.1 PetitParser

Grammars in PetitParser are specified by composing primitive parser objects using a series of overloaded operators forming an internal domain-specific language. Table 6.1 displays a comparison of the traditional PEG operators and their adaptation in primitive PetitParser objects.

Furthermore, we provide a series of other primitive parser objects that can be used to attach semantic actions to grammars and some convenience methods that help efficient whitespace consumption and token creation. These actions are listed in Table 6.2.

For example, the grammar of identifiers is implemented as follows:

PEG Operator	PetitParser	Description
'a'	`$a asParser`	Literal character
"ab"	`'ab' asParser`	Literal string
[a-z]	`$a - $z`	Character class
	`#letter asParser`	Named character class
(e)	`(e)`	Grouping
e?	`e optional`	Optional
e*	`e star`	Zero-or-more
e+	`e plus`	One-or-more
&e	`e and`	And-predicate
!e	`e not`	Not-predicate
e1 e2	`e1 , e2`	Sequence
e1 / e2	`e1 / e2`	Ordered choice

Table 6.1: The primitive PEG operators and their counterpart in PetitParser.

PetitParser	Description
`e ==> aBlock`	Attach semantic action aBlock to e
`e trim`	Consume whitespace around e
`e token`	Create token of e
`e end`	Expect end of input after e

Table 6.2: Additional convenience constructors in PetitParser.

```
identifier := #letter asParser , (#letter asParser / #digit asParser) star.
```

The expressions `#letter asParser` and `#digit asParser` return parsers that accept a single character of the respective character class; the ',' operator combines two parsers to a sequence; the '/' operator combines two parsers to an ordered choice; and the 'star' operator accepts zero or more instances of another parser. As a result we end up with a graph of connected parser objects that can be used to parse input:

```
identifier parse: 'id12'.          "consumes input and returns a default AST"
identifier parse: '123'.      "returns parse failure: letter expected at 1"
```

At all times the graph of parser objects remains accessible and mutable. An existing composite parser object can be further used to build more complex languages. We are able to recompose, transform and change an existing grammar, as we shall see in upcoming examples.

6.2 PetitParser in Practice

In this section we use the Smalltalk grammar as the running example. It is the same grammar used in the Language Box implementation presented in Chapter 5. The grammar consists of 242 primitive parser objects that are grouped into 78 productions. One of these productions is the identifier rule we have seen in the previous section. The parser produces a standard Smalltalk AST and passes all 296 unit tests of the original hand-written parser.

6.2.1 Grammar Specialization

Although complex grammars can be defined using a script, we provide a convenient way to define grammars as part of a class. Each production is implemented using an instance variable and a method returning the grammar of the rule. Productions within the grammar are referred to by accessing the instance variable. This allows us to resolve mutually recursive productions by initializing all slots with a forward reference that is resolved by subsequently calling the production methods [Bracha, 2007].

Furthermore, defining grammars in classes enables developers to take advantage of the existing development tools. Additionally, we gain the ability to extend grammars by subclassing. For example, the Smalltalk grammar is split into various classes inheriting from SmalltalkGrammar, which defines the language grammar only. The subclass SmalltalkParser adds production actions to build the abstract syntax-tree (AST):

```
SmalltalkGrammar>>variable
    ^ identifier
```

```
SmalltalkParser>>variable
    ^ super identifier ==> [ :token | VariableNode token: token ]
```

Subclassing gives us the possibility to reuse the same grammar with different tools, such as compiler, editor (syntax highlighting, code completion) and debugger (code evaluation).

6.2.2 Grammar Composition

PetitParser is built around composition: simple parsers are combined into more complex ones. Grammars can arbitrarily be reused and composed. For example to reuse the grammar for a Smalltalk method declaration, we can ask for its production, which is a working parser by itself. Furthermore we can then combine this production with the grammar of another language, such as SQL:

```
SmalltalkGrammar new methodDeclaration , SqlGrammar new.
```

As presented in Chapter 5, Language Boxes implement an adaptive language model for fine-grained language changes and language composition. The Language Box implementation is built on top of PetitParser and performs a dynamic grammar composition of the host language and the language extensions active in the given compilation context.

Composing grammars is difficult using traditional table based grammars, as the tables need to be merged while resolving possible conflicts. Dynamically recompiling table based grammars is often not viable due to space and time concerns.

6.2.3 Grammar Conflicts

The downside to being able to arbitrarily compose grammars is that this might lead to subtle problems. In the following example we reuse the language extension from Section 5.1 that makes it possible to put SQL expressions anywhere in Smalltalk code. The problem in this example is that the embedded SQL expression could also be parsed as a valid Smalltalk expression[1]:

```
Person>>load
    ^ SELECT * FROM "Person"
```

While the parse is always unambiguous (because of the ordered choice), the result of the above expression depends on the order in which the two languages have been composed. In the previous chapter we argued that this specific language embedding is relatively safe, since SQL is a restrictive language that cannot parse typical Smalltalk expressions. While this works well in practice for this particular example, it might not be feasible for other examples. Emerging problems might stay unnoticed and cause programmatically composed grammars to behave in unexpected ways.

To avoid this problem we introduced an unordered choice at the merge points. This enforces that exactly one of the two grammar fragments parses. Interestingly, the unordered choice '|' is trivial to implement using the semantic negation predicate '!' of PEG parsers:

---

1 In Smalltalk the expression would represent the multiplication of the variables SELECT and FROM, and " Person" would be a comment.

```
Parser>>| aParser
    "Answer a new parser that either parses the receiver or aParser, fail if both
    pass (exclusive or)."

    ^ (self not , aParser) / (aParser not , self)
```

The resulting parser enforces that exactly one of the two choices parses. Contrary to the unordered choice in CFGs our implementation does not work statically at compile-time, but dynamically at parse-time. Note that the unordered choice should not be used as the default choice operator as its use leads to exponential parse times: both choices are followed on each parse.

On top of the unordered choice we can define other operators, such as a `dynamicChoice:`. This operator lets the user disambiguate and potentially change the grammar on-the-fly:

```
Parser>>dynamicChoice: aParser
    ^ self | aParser / [ :stream |
      | resolution |
      resolution := UIManager default
        chooseFrom: { self name. aParser name }
        values: { self. aParser }
        title: 'Resolve ambiguity at ' , stream position asString.
      resolution parseOn: stream ] asParser
```

With these extensions, the difference between CFGs and PetitParser is similar to the difference between statically and dynamically typed languages. In both PetitParser and dynamically typed languages, static errors (such as grammar ambiguities or type errors) are detected at runtime only, at the gain of additional flexibility at run-time [Meijer and Drayton, 2004]. This flexibility is needed to support Language Boxes where different grammars need to be composed that might not have been designed to work together.

6.2.4 Grammar Transformations

The ability to transform grammars is powerful and goes beyond static extensibility by single inheritance: transformations can be applied on-demand and multiple transformations can be chained.

To highlight code, we can instantiate the basic grammar definition and wrap all parsers that create a token with an action block that highlights the character range in the editor. The backtracking occurring during the parse is not a problem, because the method `highlight:range:` overrides the style if set previously. In any case the highlighting purely happens as a side-effect of the parsing.

```
grammar := SmalltalkGrammar new.
highlighter := grammar transform: [ :parser |
    parser class = TokenParser
        ifTrue: [ parser ==> [ :token |
            anEditor highlight: token style range: token interval ] ]
        ifFalse: [ parser ] ].
```

The `transform:` method walks over the complete grammar, replacing each matching parser with the result of evaluating the transformation block. Here, token parsers are transformed to perform the highlighting action.

A problem with this solution is that highlighting only works for valid source code, and stops after the first syntax error. With another transformation we can make the grammar "fuzzy" and try to skip to the next statement separator in case an error arises while parsing expressions:

```
fuzzyHighlighter := highlighter transform: [ :parser |
    parser name = #expression
        ifTrue: [ parser / [ :stream | stream upTo: $. ] asParser ]
        ifFalse: [ parser ] ].
```

In a similar manner other kinds of common errors can be skipped, and the user can be warned while writing the code.

PetitParser also provides a query interface to reflect on parsers:

- `aParser allParsers` returns a collection of all parsers in the grammar;

- `aParser allTerminals` returns a collection of all terminal parsers in the grammar;

- `aParser firstSet` returns the terminal parsers that consume input first in `aParser`;

- `aParser followSet` returns the parsers that follow `aParser`; and

- `aParser cycleSet` returns a set of all parsers that are within one or more cycles of left-recursion.

We can combine the transformation techniques and the reflective facilities to dynamically generate a grammar to answer other questions, such as what could possibly follow at a specific point in a source file:

```
PPParser>>whatFollows: aString at: anInteger
   | stream |
   stream := aString asPetitStream.
   (self transform: [ :parser |
      parser ==> [ :node |
         stream position < anInteger
            ifTrue: [ node ]
            ifFalse: [ ^ parser followSet ] ] ])
      parseOn: stream.
   ^ #()
```

6.2.5 Declarative Grammar Rewriting

Grammars can furthermore be searched and transformed using a declarative graph transformation engine. We have used this tool to optimize grammars. The following example illustrates the implementation of such an optimization rule: it removes duplicated parsers within an ordered choice:

```
1 duplicatedParser := PPPattern any.
2 beforeList := PPListPattern any.
3 betweenList := PPListPattern any.
4 afterList := PPListPattern any.
5
6 rewriter := Rewriter new.
7 rewriter
8    replace: beforeList / duplicatedParser / betweenList / duplicatedParser /
         afterList
9    with: beforeList / duplicatedParser / betweenList / afterList.
10 rewriter execute: grammar
```

Lines 1–4 instantiate four parser patterns: `duplicatedParser` matches any primitive parser object; and `beforeList`, `betweenList`, and `afterList` match any (possibly empty) list of parsers. On line 6 the grammar rewriter is instantiated and on lines 7–9 the replacement is defined. The transformation of the grammar is started on line 10.

The rewriter traverses over the complete grammar trying to match the pattern (line 8). We are using an unification algorithm on the grammar graph that tries to substitute the patterns in the search expression with actual parsers from the grammar to be transformed. In this example the pattern `duplicatedParser` appears twice.

It enforces the same parser to appear twice in the choice. If a match is found, the replacement rule is instantiated with the matched parsers and inserted into the grammar.

The declarative grammar rewriting is used internally in the Language Box implementation to compose and transform the different grammars. While our original implementation used an imperative approach, the declarative rewriting is simpler and easier to understand.

Furthermore, we have defined a series of grammar normalizations [Lämmel and Zaytsev, 2010] and optimizations similar to the ones implemented in *Rats!* [Grimm, 2006]. We could not measure a notable speed improvement for hand written grammars. However the optimizations do normalize and thus provide a notable performance improvement on grammars that have degraded because of programmatic composition and transformation operations, such as the ones happening with Language Boxes.

6.2.6 Tool Support

Figure 6.1 displays the a grammar workspace which provides a rich set of static and dynamic tools that directly work on the object model of PetitParser.

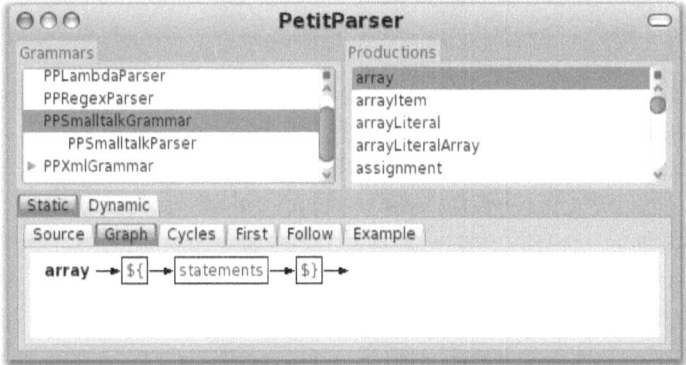

Figure 6.1: The PetitParser grammar workspace displaying the currently selected production.

The static tools consist of all elements that work on the specification of the grammar. The *source* tab enables editing of productions; the *graph* tab displays the graphical structure of productions; the *example* tab displays random examples for the selected production, which is useful to spot errors in the grammar definition; the *cycles* tab lists direct cycles that could cause inefficient grammars; and the *first* and *follow* tabs display the respective set of parsers that consume input first and that follow the selected production.

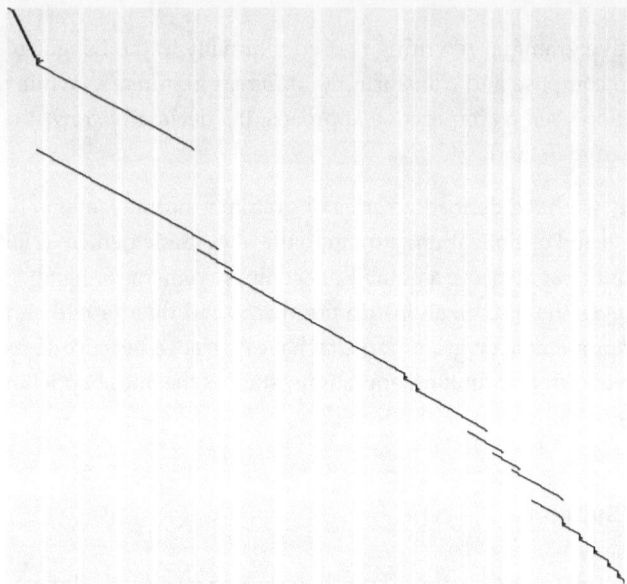

Figure 6.2: Progress of an example parse with backtracking in choice operator.

The dynamic tools work on the currently selected production and an input to parse: The *parse* tab displays and optionally opens an inspector on the resulting AST; the *tally* tab displays the absolute and relative activation count of each production; the *profile* tab displays absolute and relative time spent in each production; the *progress* tab visualizes the progress of the parser through the input — from left-to-right the input string is depicted (whitespaces in white), from top-to bottom the time (see Figure 6.2); and the *debugger* tab gives the possibility to step forwards and backwards through the input while highlighting the consumed text and the active productions.

6.2.7 Performance

Parser Combinators, PEGs, and even Packrat parsers are often accused of being slow, due to their dynamic nature. Our experience has shown the contrary: when the grammar is carefully written PetitParser can compete with a highly optimized LALR table based parser. Efficient grammars can be achieved with automatic grammar optimization transformations (Section 6.2.5) and the help of the static and dynamic tools (Section 6.2.6).

Parser	characters/sec
Hand-Written Parser	553 492
PetitParser	138 053
LALR Parser	122 888

Table 6.3: Average throughput in characters per second parsing the Smalltalk collection hierarchy on a MacBook Pro 2.8 GHz Intel Core 2 Duo.

In Table 6.3 we list the average throughput of different Smalltalk parsers producing an identical AST. The hand-written recursive descent parser is a clear winner, being almost 5 times as fast as the other two parsers.

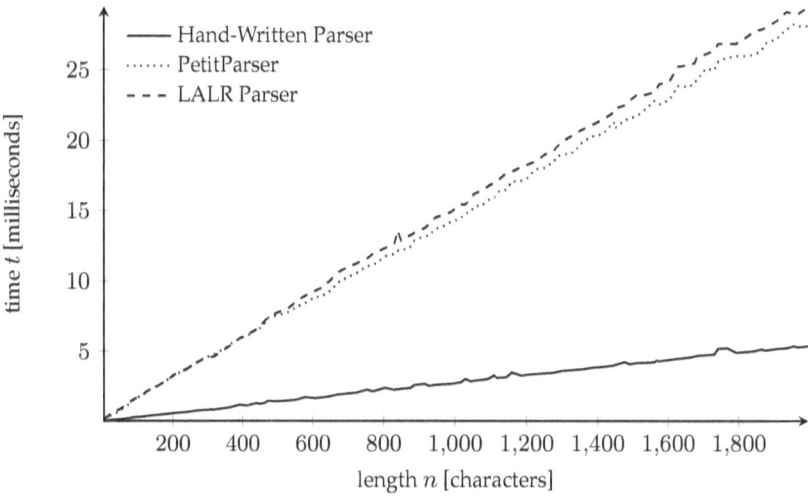

Figure 6.3: Parsing time t in milliseconds of Smalltalk code of increasing input size n in characters on a MacBook Pro 2.8 GHz Intel Core 2 Duo.

In Figure 6.3 we depict the parsing time of the same parsers with increasing input size. To generate comparable results we started with an empty method and incrementally added random code statements to the method body. This reveals the linear parse-time of each benchmarked parser with increasing input size.

We expected the LALR parser to perform better, given the sophisticated optimization algorithms implemented in this compiler-compiler. Profiling the parsers reveals that the LALR parser spends most of its time looking up, decoding and dispatching values from its tables. PetitParser on the other hand shows a deep nesting of message sends. This is something a dynamic language like Smalltalk can do very efficiently.

6.3 Related Work

OMeta [Warth and Piumarta, 2007] is an object-oriented pattern matcher based on a variant of PEGs. OMeta uses itself to transform grammar specifications to host language code. *Rats!* [Grimm, 2006] is a packrat parser framework that provides a sophisticated infrastructure to transform and to optimize grammars using the visitor design pattern. Both frameworks support grammar composition, but due to their code generation make it impossible to change the grammar after compilation.

Various other object-oriented frameworks for parser combinators have been proposed: *JParsec, Scala Parser Combinators* [Moors *et al.*, 2008], and *Newspeak* [Bracha, 2007]. All implementations use the host language to build an object model of parser objects. Extensibility is achieved through subclassing or mixing mechanisms of the respective host languages. Although we expect that grammar transformations are possible on these models, we are unaware if this has actually been done in practice.

Composing and reusing table based parsers is an ongoing research topic [Heering *et al.*, 1989; Brabranda and Schwartzbach, 2007; Bravenboer and Visser, 2009]. All approaches have limitations in composability and can be described as difficult at best. Grammar changes require an expensive recompilation of the new grammar. Schwerdfeger *et al.* [Schwerdfeger and Wyk, 2010] propose a solution to efficiently compose table based grammars at specific extension points.

6.4 Conclusion

In this chapter we motivated the use of dynamic grammars. We have presented several examples and some basic performance analysis that demonstrate the usefulness of having 'late-bound' grammars where everything is accessible and changeable at runtime.

The Language Box infrastructure depends on the ability to dynamically transform and change grammars. Furthermore, the dynamic grammars do not impose limitations on composability and allow us to resolve possible conflicts at parse-time, something that is not supported in the related work.

Chapter 7

Domain-Specific Program Checking

> *"A successful [software] tool is one that was used to do something undreamed of by its author."*
> — Stephen C. Johnson

Lint-like program checkers are popular tools that ensure code quality by verifying compliance with best practices for a particular programming language. The proliferation of internal domain-specific languages and models, however, poses new challenges for such tools. Traditional program checkers produce many false positives and fail to accurately check constraints, best practices, common errors, possible optimizations and portability issues *particular to domain-specific languages*.

In this chapter we advocate the use of dedicated rules to check domain-specific practices using the Helvetia toolchain. We demonstrate the implementation of domain-specific rules, the automatic repair of violations, and their application to two case-studies: (1) Seaside defines several internal DSLs through a creative use of the syntax of the host language; and (2) Magritte adds meta-descriptions to existing code by means of special methods. Our empirical validation demonstrates that domain-specific program checking significantly improves code quality when compared with general-purpose program checking.

7.1 History of Program Checking

The use of automatic program checkers to statically locate possible bugs and other problems in source code has a long history. While the first program checkers were part of the compiler, later on separate tools were written that performed more sophisticated analyses of code to detect possible problem patterns [Johnson, 1978]. The refactoring book [Fowler, 1999] made code smell detection popular as an indicator to decide when and what to refactor.

Most modern development environments (IDEs) directly provide lint-like tools as part of their editors to warn developers about emerging problems in their source code. These checkers usually highlight offending code snippets on-the-fly and greatly enhance the quality of the written code. Contrary to a separate tool, IDEs with integrated program checkers encourage developers to write good code right from the beginning. Today's program checkers [Hovemeyer and Pugh, 2004] reliably detect issues like possible bugs, portability issues, violations of coding conventions, duplicated, dead, or suboptimal code, *etc.*

Many software projects today use *domain-specific languages* (DSLs) to raise the expressiveness of the host language in a particular problem domain. A common approach is to derive a new pseudo-language from an existing API. This technique is known as a *Fluent Interface*, a form of an *internal domain-specific language* or *embedded language* [Fowler, 2010]. Such languages are syntactically compatible with the host language and use the same compiler and the same runtime infrastructure.

As such, DSLs often make creative use of host language features with atypical use of its syntax. This confuses traditional program checkers and results in many false positives. For example, chains of method invocations are normally considered bad practice as they expose internal implementation details and violate the Law of Demeter [Lieberherr, 1989]. However in internal DSLs, method chaining is a commonly applied technique to invoke a sequence of calls on the same object where each call returns the receiver object for further calls. In other words, the DSL *abstracts* from the traditional use of the host language and introduces new idioms that are meaningful in the particular problem domain.

Figure 7.1 depicts the dimensions of program checking: Traditional program checkers work at the level of source code, see Figure 7.1(a). Tools like *intensional views* [Mens *et al.*, 2006] and *reflexion models* [Murphy *et al.*, 1995; Koschke and Simon, 2003] check for structural irregularities and for conformance at an architectural level, see Figure 7.1(b). Furthermore, tools like *PathFinder* [Havelund and Pressburger, 2000] have been used to transform source code into a model and apply model checking algorithms.

We argue that a new dimension of program checking and a different set of rules are necessary as developers *abstract from their host language*. Standard program checking tools are not effective when it comes to detecting problems in domain-specific code. In this chapter we advocate the use of dedicated program checking rules that

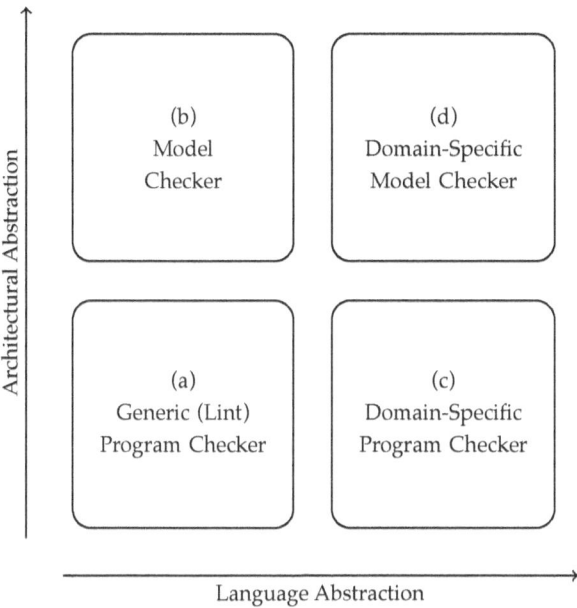

Figure 7.1: Dimensions of program checking.

know about and check for the specific use-cases of (internal) domain-specific languages. As with traditional rules this can happen at the level of the source code, see Figure 7.1(c); or at a higher architectural or modeling level, see Figure 7.1(d).

We will demonstrate two rule-sets which both abstract from the traditional host language use and work at different level of architectural abstraction:

1. Seaside is an open-source web application framework written in Smalltalk [Ducasse *et al.*, 2007]. Seaside defines various internal DSLs to configure application settings, nest components, define the flow of pages, and generate XHTML. As part of our work as Seaside maintainers and as software consultants on various industrial Seaside projects, we developed *Slime*, a Seaside-specific program checker consisting of a set of 30 rules working at the level of the abstract syntax tree (AST). We analyze the impact of these rules on a long term evolution of Seaside itself and of applications built on top of it.

2. Magritte is a recursive metamodel integrated into the reflective metamodel of Smalltalk [Renggli *et al.*, 2007]. The metamodel of an application is specified by implementing annotated methods that are automatically called by Magritte to build a representative metamodel of the system. This metamodel is then used to automate various tasks such as editor construction, data validation, and persistency. The Magritte metamodel is specified in source code

using an internal DLS and thus is not automatically verified. We have implemented a set of 5 rules that validate a Magritte metamodel against its meta-metamodel.

Our approach builds on top of the Helvetia engine to cleanly extend the development environment with domain-specific program checking facilities. It reuses the existing toolchain of editor, parser, compiler and debugger by leveraging the AST of the host environment. While Helvetia is applicable in a much broader context, in this chapter we focus on the program analysis and transformation part of it.

Detection rules are declaratively specified using AST pattern matching, as introduced in Section 4.1.2. This technical aspect for program checking is not new. However, our approach builds on that and offers a way to specify declaratively domain-specific rules with possible automatic transformations.

The chapter is structured as follows: Section 7.2 introduces the different rule-sets we have implemented. We present the internal domain-specific languages addressed by our rules, and we discuss how we implemented and integrated the rules. In Section 7.3 we report on our experience of applying these rules on various open-source and commercial systems. Furthermore we present a user survey where we asked developers to compare domain-specific rules with traditional ones. Section 7.4 discusses related work and Section 7.5 concludes.

7.2 Examples of Domain-Specific Rules

In this section we demonstrate two sets of rules at different levels of abstraction: while the first set of rules (Section 7.2.1) works directly on the source code of web applications, the second set of rules (Section 7.2.2) uses a metamodel and validates it against the system. While in both cases the source code is normal Smalltalk, we focus on the domain-specific use of the language in these two contexts.

7.2.1 Syntactic rules for Seaside

The most prominent use of an internal DSL in Seaside is the generation of HTML. This DSL is built around a stream-like object that understands messages to create different XHTML tags. Furthermore the tag objects understand messages to add the HTML attributes to the generated markup. These attributes are specified using a chain of message sends, known in the Smalltalk jargon as a cascade:

```
1  html div
2    class: 'large';
3    with: count.
4  html anchor
5    callback: [ count := count + 1 ];
6    with: 'increment'.
```

The above code creates the following HTML markup:

```
<div class="large">0</div>
<a src="/?_s=28hVYPUhdMM7mU&1">increment</a>
```

Lines 1–3 are responsible for the generation of the div tag with the CSS class large and the value of the current count as the contents of the tag. Lines 4–6 generate the link with the label *increment*. The src attribute is provided by Seaside. Clicking the link automatically evaluates the code on line 5 and redisplays the component.

This *little language* [Deursen and Klint, 1997] for HTML generation is the most prominent use of a DSL in Seaside. It lets developers abstract common HTML patterns into convenient methods rather than pasting the same sequence of tags into templates every time.

As developers and users of Seaside, we have observed that while the HTML generation is simple, there are a few common problems that repeatedly appear in the source code of contributors. We have collected these problems and categorized them into 4 groups: possible bugs, non-portable code between different Smalltalk platforms, bad style, and suboptimal code. Spotting such problems early in the development cycle can significantly improve the code quality, maintainability, and might avoid hard to detect bugs. We list all the rules and detail on the implementation of one rule per group.

Possible Bugs. This group of rules detects severe problems that are most certainly serious bugs in the source code:

- The message with: is not last in the cascade,

- Instantiates new component while generating HTML,

- Manually invokes renderContentOn:,

- Uses the wrong output stream,

- Misses call to super implementation,

- Calls functionality not available while generating output, and

- Calls functionality not available within a framework callback.

To illustrate such a rule, we take a closer look at "The message with: is not last in the cascade". While in most cases it does not matter in which order the attributes of a HTML tag are specified, Seaside requires the children of a tag to be specified last using with:. This allows Seaside to directly stream the tags to the socket, without having to build an intermediate tree of DOM nodes. In the erroneous code below the order is reversed:

```
html div
    with: count;
    class: 'large'.
```

One might argue that the design of the DSL could avoid this ordering problem in the first place. However, in the case of Seaside, we reuse the existing syntax of the host language and we cannot change and add additional validation into the compiler, otherwise this would not be an internal DSL anymore.

Slime uses the Helvetia rule system (Section 3.1.3) to declaratively specify its rules. Helvetia collects the rules annotated with <programchecker> and automatically applies them whenever source code changes. The following code snippet demonstrates the complete code necessary to implement the rule to check whether with: is the last message in the cascade:

```
1  CheckerRuleDatabase>>withHasToBeLastInCascade
2     <programchecker>
3     ^ CheckerRule new
4        label: 'The message with: has to be last in the cascade';
5        search: (ConditionRule new
6           if: [ :context | context isHtmlGeneratingMethod ]
7           then: (TreeRule new
8              expression: '`html `message with: ``@arguments';
9              condition: [ :node |
10                node parent isCascade and: [ node isLastMessage not ] ]));
```

Line 3 instantiates the rule object, line 4 assigns a label that appears in the user interface and lines 5–10 define the actual search pattern.

The precondition on line 5 asserts statically that the code artifact under test is used by Seaside to generate HTML. The ConditionRule object lets developers scope rules to relevant parts of the software using the reflective API of the host language. This

```
          TreeRule
                           `html `message with: ``@arguments


                  `html                `message:              ``
@arguments                              ``@arguments
```

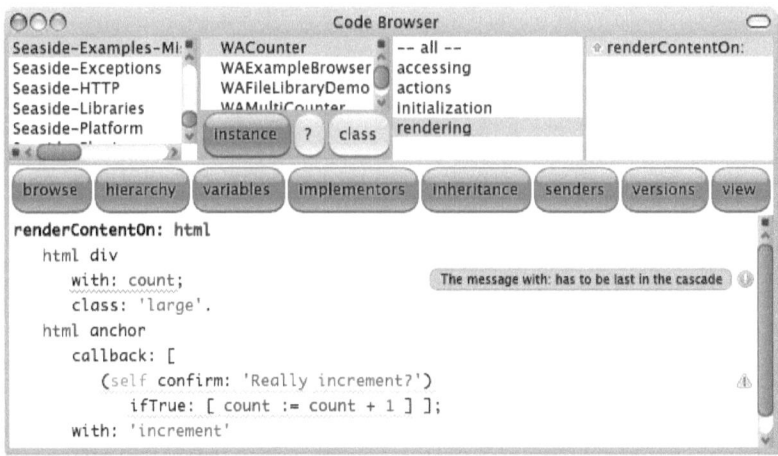

Figure 7.2:

```
replace: [ :node |
    node cascade
        remove: node;
        addLast: node ].
```

Lines 13 and 14 remove the matched node from the cascade and add it back to the end of the sequence. After applying the transformation, Helvetia automatically reruns the search to ensure that the transformation actually resolves the problem.

Again the tools from the IDE automatically offer the possibility to trigger such an automatic transformation. For example, when a developer right-clicks on a Slime issue in the "Code Browser" a confirmation dialog with a preview is presented before the transformation is applied. Furthermore it is possible to ignore and mark false positives, so that they do not show up again.

Bad style. These rules detect some less severe problems that might pose maintainability problems in the future but that do not cause immediate bugs. An example of such a rule is "Extract callback code to separate method". As shown below, the rule proposes to extract the code within the callback into a separate method. This ensures that code related to controller functionality is kept separate from the view.

```
html anchor
   callback: [
      (self confirm: 'Really increment?')
         ifTrue: [ count := count + 1 ] ];
   with: 'increment'.
```

Other rules in this category include:

- Use of deprecated API, and

- Non-standard object initialization.

The implementation of these rules is similar to the one demonstrated in the previous section on "possible bugs".

Suboptimal Code. This set of rules suggests optimizations that can be applied to code without changing its behavior. The following code triggers the rule "Unnecessary block passed to brush":

```
html div with: [ html text: count ]
```

The code could be rewritten as follows, but this triggers the rule "Unnecessary #with: sent to brush":

```
html div with: count
```

This in turn can be rewritten to the following code which is equivalent to the first version, but much shorter and more efficient as no block closure is activated:

```
html div: count
```

Non-Portable Code.   While this set of rules is less important for application code, it is essential for the Seaside code base itself. The framework runs without modification on 7 different platforms (Pharo Smalltalk, Squeak Smalltalk, Cincom Smalltalk, GemStone Smalltalk, VA Smalltalk, GNU Smalltalk and Dolphin Smalltalk), which slightly differ in both the syntax and the libraries they support. To avoid that contributors using a specific platform accidentally submit code which only works on their platform, we have added a number of rules that check for compatibility:

- Invalid object initialization,
- Uses curly brace arrays,
- Uses literal byte arrays,
- Uses method annotations,
- Uses non-portable class,
- Uses non-portable message,
- ANSI booleans,
- ANSI collections,
- ANSI conditionals,
- ANSI convertor,
- ANSI exceptions, and
- ANSI streams.

Code like `count asString` might not run on all platforms identically, as the convertor method `asString` is not part of the common protocol. Thus, if the code is run on a platform that does not implement `asString` the code might break or produce unexpected results.

The implementation and the automatic refactoring for this issue is particularly simple:

```
1  CheckerRuleDatabase>>nonPortableMessage
2     <programchecker>
3     ^ CheckerRule new
4        label: 'Uses non-portable message';
5        search: '``@obj asString' replace: '``@obj seasideString';
6        search: '``@obj asInteger' replace: '``@obj seasideInteger'
```

Again the rule is defined in the class CheckerRuleDatabase. It consists of two matching patterns (line 5 and 6 respectively) and their associated transformation, so code like count asString will be transformed to count seasideString.

7.2.2 Magritte — code checking with a metamodel

Constraint checking is not a new domain. Classic approaches rely on constraints that are specified by the analyst [Mens *et al.*, 2006; Murphy *et al.*, 1995; Koschke and Simon, 2003] and that are checked against the actual application code. In this case these rules are external to the execution of the program. Model-driven designs often rely on a metamodel to add more semantics to the code by providing transformations that are either statically (via code generation) or dynamically interpreted. These metamodels come with a set of constraints that can also be used for checking the program.

Magritte is a metamodel that is used to automate various tasks such as editor building, data validation and persistency [Renggli *et al.*, 2007]. In this section we detail its use and the rules that can be derived from the constraints it imposes.

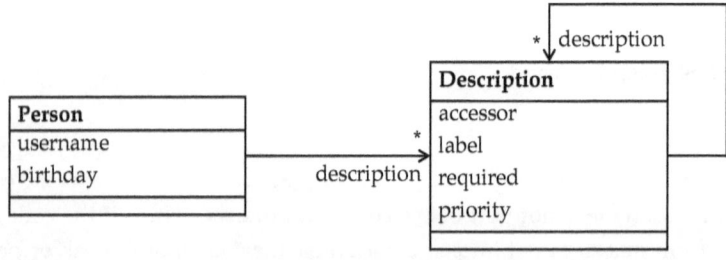

Figure 7.3: The domain object Person with its Magritte meta-description.

On the left side of Figure 7.3 we see a simple domain class called Person with two attributes. To meta-describe a class with Magritte we need corresponding description instances. These description instances are either defined in the source-code or dynamically at runtime. The following code shows an example of how we could describe the attribute username in the class Person:

```
1  Person class>>usernameDescription
2      <description>
3      ^ StringDescription new
4          accessor: #username;
5          label: 'Username';
6          beRequired;
7          yourself
```

The method returns an attribute description of the type string (line 3), that can be accessed through the method #username (line 4), which has the label 'Username' (line 5), and is a required property (line 6). The annotation (line 2) lets Magritte know that calling the method returns a description of the receiver. Several such description methods build the metamodel of the Person class as visualized with the association from Person to Description in Figure 7.3.

Descriptions are interpreted by different services, such as form builders or persistency mappers. For example, a simple renderer that prints the label and the current values would look like this:

```
1  aPerson description do: [ :desc |
2      aStream
3          nextPutAll: (desc label);
4          nextPutAll: ': ';
5          nextPutAll: (desc toString: (desc accessor readFrom: aPerson));
6          cr ]
```

First, given an aPerson instance, we ask it for its description and we iterate over its individual attribute descriptions (line 1). Within the loop, we print the label (line 3), we ask the accessor of the description to return the associated attributes from aPerson and we transform this value to a string (line 5), so that it can be appended to the output.

In the remainder of this section we present how we check the proper use of Magritte using Magritte itself. We have defined five rules which check for conformance of the source code with the Magritte metamodel.

The first two rules are defined and implemented externally to the Magritte engine:

1. Description Naming. The definitions of the attribute descriptions should relate to the accessor they describe. In our example the accessor is username and the method that defines the description is called `usernameDescription`. While this is not a strict requirement, it is considered good style and makes the code easier to read. The implementation points out places where this practice is neglected.

2. Missing Description. Developers sometimes fail to completely describe their classes. This rule checks all described classes of the system and compares them with the metamodel. Instance variables and accessor methods that miss a corresponding description method are reported.

The remaining three rules completely rely on the constraints already imposed by the runtime of Magritte:

3. Description Priorities. In Magritte attribute descriptions can have priorities. This is useful to have a deterministic order when elements are displayed in a user interface. This rule verifies that if a description is used to build user-interfaces then it should have valid priorities assigned to all its attribute descriptions. This rule makes use of the metamodel as well as the reflective system to detect the places where the descriptions are used.

4. Accessor Definition. The Magritte metamodel uses accessor objects to specify how the data in the model can be read and written. This rule iterates over the complete metamodel and checks the accessor object of every description against the code it is supposed to work on. The implementation of the rule is straight forward as it merely delegates to the description instance of the class under scrutiny:

```
MagritteRuleDatabase>>accessorDefinition
  <programchecker>
  ^ CheckerRule new
    label: 'Accessor Definition';
    onDescription: [ :context |
      (context accessor canReadFromInstancesOf: context theClass)
        and: [ context accessor canWriteToInstancesOf: context theClass ] ]
```

5. Description Definition. This rule checks if the specified metamodel can be properly instantiated and, if so, it validates the metamodel against its meta-metamodel. Magritte allows one to check any model against its metamodel, so we can validate `aPerson` against its metamodel:

```
aPerson description validate: aPerson
```

Magritte is described in itself as depicted in Figure 7.3. Therefore we can use the meta-metamodel to validate the metamodel in the same way:

```
MagritteRuleDatabase>>definitionDefinition
   <programchecker>
   ^ CheckerRule new
      label: 'Description Definition';
      onDescription: [ :context |
        context description description
           validate: context description ]
```

The above code validates `description` against the description of itself. In case of problems they are recorded by the program checker. In fact this rule is the most powerful of all rules presented here, because it can detect various kinds of different problems in the metamodel, yet it is extremely simple in the implementation as all the functionality is already present in Magritte.

We have developed a similar set of rules for FAME [Kuhn and Verwaest, 2008], a meta-modeling library which is independent of the host language and keeps the metamodels accessible and adaptable at runtime.

7.3 Case Studies

In this section we present three case studies: In the first two we apply Slime rules to control the code quality. The first one is Seaside itself (Section 7.3.1). The second one is a commercial application based on Seaside (Section 7.3.2). We analyze several versions of these systems and we compare the results with the number of issues detected by traditional lint rules. Then we present a survey we ran with Seaside developers concerning their experience with using the Seaside program checker (Section 7.3.3). In the third case study we apply the Magritte rules on a large collection of open-source code (Section 7.3.4) and demonstrate some common issues that remained unnoticed in the code.

7.3.1 Seaside

Figure 7.4 depicts the average number of issues over various versions of Seaside. The blue line shows the number of standard smells per class (Lint), while the orange

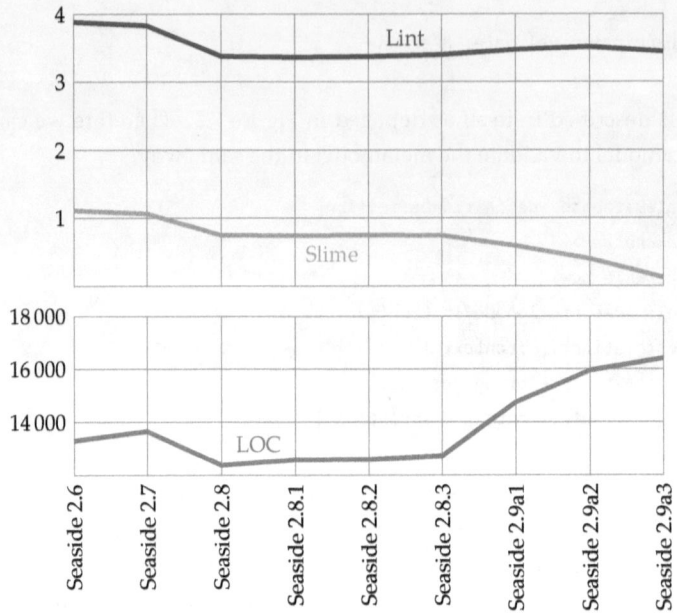

Figure 7.4: Average number of Lint and Slime issues per class (above) and lines of code (below) in released Seaside versions.

line shows the number of domain-specific smells per class (Slime). To give a feeling of how the size of the code base changes in time, we also display the number of lines of code (LOC) below.

In both cases we observe a improvement in code quality between versions 2.7 and 2.8. At the time major parts of Seaside were refactored or rewritten to increase portability and extensibility of the code base. No changes are visible for the various 2.8 releases. Code quality as measured by the program checkers and lines of code remained constant over time.

Starting with Seaside 2.9a1 Slime was introduced in the development process. While the quality as measured by the traditional lint rules remained constant, guiding development by the Slime rules significantly improved the quality of the domain-specific code. This particular period shows the value in domain-specific program checking. While the Seaside code base grew significantly, the number of Slime rules could be reduced to almost zero.

Feedback we got from early adopters of Seaside 2.9 confirms that the quality of the code is notably better. Especially the portability between different Smalltalk dialects has improved. The code typically compiles and passes the tests on all platforms even though it comes from the shared code repository.

An interesting observation is that even if the Slime smells are reduced and the quality of the code improves, the standard Lint rules continue to report a rather constant proportion of problems. This is due to the fact that the generic Lint rules address the wrong level and produce too many false positives.

We further evaluated the number of *false positives* of the remaining open issues in the last analyzed version of Seaside by manually verifying the reported issues: this is 67% (940 false positives out of 1403 issues reported) in the case of Lint, and 24% (12 false positives out of 51 issues reported) in the case of Slime. This demonstrates that applying dedicated rules provides a better report on the quality of the software than using the generic rules.

Due to the dynamic nature of Smalltalk and its lack of static type information it seems to be hard to further improve the quality of Slime rules. We do however see potential in future work to reduce the number of false positives by using static [Pluquet *et al.*, 2009] and dynamic [Denker *et al.*, 2007b] type analysis.

7.3.2 Cmsbox

The Cmsbox is a commercial web content management system written in Seaside. Figure 7.5 depicts the development of the system over three years. We are external to the development. The company gave us access to their code, but we could not correlate with their internal quality model and bug reports. Still we could deduce some interesting points: We ran the same set of Lint and Slime tests on every fifth version committed, for a total of 220 distinct versions analyzed. The number of lines of code are displayed below, though the absolute numbers have been removed to anonymize the data.

In the beginning we observe a rapid increase of detected issues. This is during the initial development phase of the project where a lot of code was added in a relatively short time. Presumably the violation of standard rules was not a concern for the developers. By contrast the number of Slime issues remained low and showed only gradual increase by comparison. This is a interesting difference. Since the Slime rules tackle the development of the web interface which was the key part of the development effort, the result shows the benefit of using domain-specific code checking: developers focus more on domain-specific issues than on the general issues that can typically be resolved much more easily.

The abrupt drop of Lint (and to some smaller extent also Slime) issues at point (a) can be explained by the removal of a big chunk of experimental or prototypical code

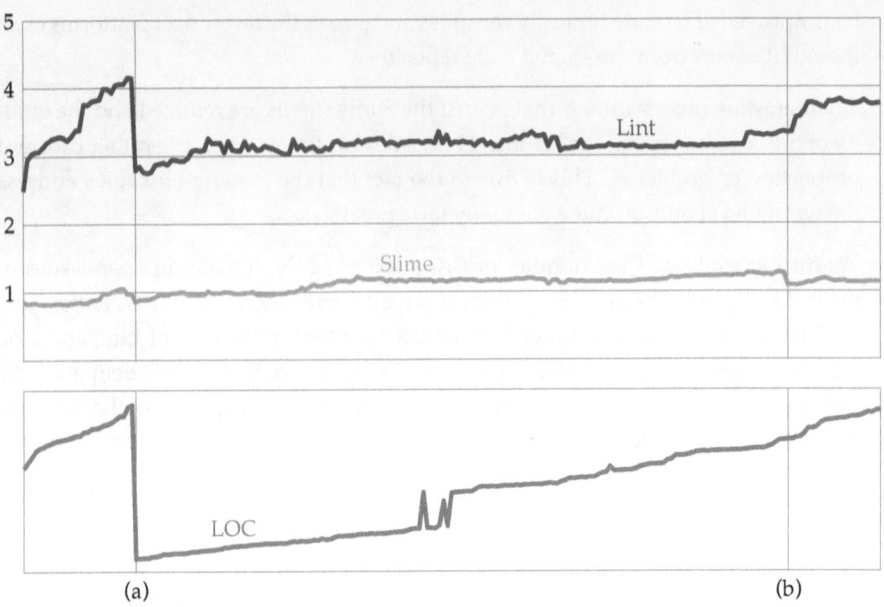

Figure 7.5: Average number of Lint and Slime issues per class (above) and lines of code (below) in 220 subsequent development versions of the Cmsbox.

no longer in use. Between versions (a) and (b) the code size grew more slowly, and the code quality remained relatively stable. It is worth noting that the size of the code base grew gradually, but at the same time the proportion of Slime issues stayed constant.

During the complete development of the Cmsbox the standard Lint rules were run as part of the daily builds. This explains why the average number of issues per class is lower than in the case of Seaside. At point (b) Slime rules were added and run with every build process. This accounts for the drop of Slime issues. A new development effort after (b) caused an increasing number of Lint issues. Again it is interesting to see that the better targeted Slime rules remained stable compared to the traditional ones.

Contrary to the case study with Seaside, the Slime issues do not disappear completely. On the one hand this has to do with the fact that the software is not supposed to run on different platforms, thus the rules that check for conformity on that level were not considered by the development team. On the other hand, as this is typical in an industrial setup, the developers were not able to spend a significant amount of time on the issues that were harder to fix and that did not cause immediate problems.

7.3.3 User Survey

We asked Seaside developers to complete a survey on Lint and Slime usage. 23 experienced Seaside developers independent from us answered our questionnaire. We asked them first to state their use of program checkers:

1. How often do you use Slime on your Seaside code?
   4 daily, 4 weekly, 8 monthly, 7 never

2. How often do you use standard code critics on your Seaside code?
   3 daily, 5 weekly, 7 monthly, 8 never

16 developers (70%) are using Slime on a regular basis. We asked these developers to give their level of agreement or disagreement on the five-point Likert scale to the following statements:

3. Slime helps me to write better Seaside code:
   11 agree, 5 strongly agree

4. Slime is more useful than standard code critics to find problems in Seaside code:
   5 neither agree nor disagree, 8 agree, 3 strongly agree

5. Slime does not produce useful results, it mostly points out code that I do not consider bad:
   3 strongly disagree, 10 disagree, 3 neither agree nor disagree

All developers that use Slime on a regular basis found it useful. 69% of the developers stated that Slime produces more useful results than the standard program checkers, the remaining 31% could not see any difference. 81% of the developers stated that Slime produces relevant results that help them to detect critical problems in their application.

Our thesis has been confirmed by the two case studies and the user survey: While the general-purpose Lint rules are definitely useful to be applied to any code base, they are not effective enough when used on domain-specific code. Using dedicated rules decreases the number of false positives and gives more relevant information on how to avoid bugs and improve the source code.

7.3.4 Magritte

In our third case study we ran the Magritte rules on a large collection of open-source code. This includes Pier, an application and content management system; Squeak-Source, a source code management system; Conrad, a conference management system; CiteZen, a bibliography toolkit; CouchDB, a database implementation, and a large number of smaller projects that are publicly available.

In total we analyzed 70 768 lines of code in 12 305 methods belonging to 1 198 classes. 307 of these classes had Magritte meta-descriptions attached, where we found a total number of 516 Magritte related issues as listed in Table 7.1.

Magritte Rule	Issues
Description Naming	37
Description Definition	78
Description Priorities	113
Accessor Definition	120
Missing Description	168

Table 7.1: Number of issues in meta-described open-source code.

The most commonly observed problem are *missing descriptions*. While this is not necessarily a bug, it shows that some authors did not completely describe their domain objects. That can either happen intentionally, because they wanted to avoid the use of Magritte in certain parts of their application, or it can happen unintentionally when they forgot to update the metamodel as they added new functionality. This rule is thus helpful when reviewing code, as it identifies code that is not properly integrated with the meta-framework.

We observed also a significant number of errors in the *description definitions*. This happens when the defined metamodel does not validate against the meta-metamodel, which can be considered a serious bug. For example, we found the following description with two problems in the Pier Blog plugin:

```
1  Blog>>descriptionItemCount
2    ^ IntegerDescription new
3      label: 'Item Count';
4      accessor: #itemCount;
5      default: 0;
6      bePositive;
7      yourself
```

First the description has no label, a required value in the meta-metamodel. The rule automatically suggests a refactoring (line 3) to add the missing label based on the name of the accessor. The second problem is the default value 0 (line 5), which does not satisfy the condition `bePositive` of the description itself (line 6).

From our positive experience with the Slime rules on the Seaside code-base, we expect a significant improvement of code quality in the realm of Magritte as these rules get adopted by the community. It is important to always keep the model and meta-model in a consistent state, which considerably improves the quality and stability of the code. With a few simple rules we can detect and fix numerous problems in the metamodel definition.

7.4 Related Program Checkers

There is a wide variety of tools available to find bugs and check for style issues. Rutar *et al.* give a good comparison of five bug finding tools for Java [Rutar *et al.*, 2004].

PMD is a program checker which includes a large collection of different rule-sets. Recent releases also included special rules to check for portability with the Android platform and common Java technologies such as J2EE, JSP, JUnit, *etc.* As such, PMD provides some domain-specific rule-sets and encourages developers to create new ones. In PMD rules are expressed either as XPath queries or using Java code. In either case, PMD provides a proprietary AST that is problematic to keep in sync with the latest Java releases. Furthermore reflective information that goes beyond a single file is not available. This is important when rules require more information on the context, such as the code defined in sub- and superclasses.

FxCop [Seela *et al.*, 2008] is a code analysis tool for .NET code assemblies that aims at ensuring best programming practices and design guidelines. While the core engine of FxCop uses symbolic analysis of class and function definitions only, the Phoenix engine adds data flow analysis on function bodies. Rules are use the reflective code model of .NET and tightly integrate with the Visual Studio IDE.

JavaCOP [Andreae *et al.*, 2006] is a pluggable type system for Java. JavaCop implements a declarative, rule-based language that works on the typed AST of the standard Sun Java compiler. As the rules are performed as part of the compilation process, JavaCOP can only reflect within the active compilation unit, this being a limitation of the Java compiler. While the framework is targeted towards customizable type systems, the authors present various examples where JavaCOP is used for domain-specific program checking. There is currently no integration with Java IDEs and no possibility to automatically refactor code.

Other tools such as *FindBugs* [Hovemeyer and Pugh, 2004] perform their analysis on bytecode. This has the advantage of being fast, but it requires that the code compile, and it completely fails to take into account the abstractions of the host language. Writing new rules is consequently very difficult (the developer needs to know how language constructs are represented as bytecode), and targeting internal DLSs is hardly possible.

The *Smalltalk Refactoring Browser* [Roberts *et al.*, 1997] includes over a hundred lint rules targeting common bugs and code smells in Smalltalk. While these rules perform well on traditional Smalltalk code, there is an increasing number of false positives when applied to domain-specific code. Helvetia and the domain-specific rules we presented in this chapter are built on top of the same infrastructure. This provides us with excellent tools for introspection and intercession of the AST in the host system, and keeps us from needing to build our own proprietary tools to parse, query and transform source code. Helvetia adds a high-level rule system to declaratively compose the rules, and to scope and integrate them into the existing development tools.

High-level abstractions can be recovered from the structural model of the code. *Intensional Views* document structural regularities in source code and check for conformance against various versions of the system [Mens *et al.*, 2006]. *Software reflexion models* [Murphy *et al.*, 1995; Koschke and Simon, 2003] extract high-level models from the source code and compare them with models the developer has specified. *ArchJava* [Aldrich *et al.*, 2002] is a language extension to Java that allows developers to encode architectural constraints directly into the source code. The constraints are checked at compile-time. Our approach does not use a special code model or architecture language to define the constraints. Instead our program checkers work with the standard code representation of the host language and make use of existing meta-frameworks such as Magritte or FAME. Furthermore, our program checker is directly integrated with the development tools.

7.5 Conclusion

In this chapter we presented how the Helvetia infrastructure was applied in the context of program checking:

1. We identified a new dimension of program checking and argued that any library providing domain-specific abstractions through embedded languages should implement a set of dedicated domain-specific rules.

2. Our empirical case studies revealed that rules that are targeted at a particular problem domain perform better and cause fewer false positives than general-purpose lint rules. While more evidence is needed, these initial case studies do point out the benefits of using rules dedicated to domain-specific code over using generic ones.

3. We presented how Helvetia makes adding domain-specific rules straightforward. It is possible to declaratively specify new Helvetia rules together with the language extensions and closely integrate them with the host environment. Furthermore the rules can be scoped to the relevant parts of the system, namely to the parts where the embedded language is active. The infrastructure of Helvetia helped us to efficiently perform searches and perform optional transformations of violations on the AST nodes of host system.

We applied the presented techniques to internal languages only. This gave us the possibility to evaluate our approach with a wide variety of real world users. As a generalization, we envision to extend this approach to any embedded language that does not necessarily share the same syntax as the host language. Since Helvetia uses the AST of the host environment as the common representation of all executable code, it is always possible to run the rules at that level. Since Helvetia automatically keeps track of the source location it is possible to highlight issues even in other languages. The challenge will be to express the rules in terms of the embedded language. This is not only necessary to be able to offer automatic transformations, but also more convenient for rule developers as they do not need to work on different abstraction levels.

Chapter 8

Host Language Requirements

*"A good programming language is
a conceptual universe for thinking
about programming."*

— Alan Perlis

Integration of multiple languages into each other and into an existing development environment is a difficult task. As a consequence, developers often end up using only internal DSLs that strictly rely on the constraints imposed by the host language. Infrastructures do exist to mix languages, but in many cases they do it at the price of losing the development tools of the host language. Instead of inventing a completely new infrastructure, our solution is to integrate new languages deeply into the existing host environment and reuse the infrastructure offered by it.

In this chapter we present the requirements and the impact of the host language choice for a system like Helvetia. We evaluate seven general-purpose languages (C++, C#, Java, Javascript, Lisp, Ruby, and Smalltalk) from the point of view of the mechanisms they offer for language integration.

The chapter is structured as follows: Section 8.1 summarizes the requirements for language embedding as we identified them in Section 1.2. Section 8.2 lists the requirements for a host environment to support a language workbench like Helvetia; and in Section 8.3 we discuss the requirements in the context of each of the proposed general-purpose languages. Section 8.4 concludes the chapter.

8.1 Requirements for Language Embedding

As a running example in this chapter we use the Extended Backus-Naur Form
[Wirth, 1977], as a simple language extension to an existing host language. The
possibility to use the EBNF directly within the code of the host language improves
the conciseness of a parser definition considerably. An example grammar to parse
numbers might look like this:

```
digit = "0" | "1" | ... | "9" ;
number = [ "-" ] digit { digit } [ "." digit { digit } ] ;
```

With the increasing demand to combine multiple languages within a single project,
different solutions have been proposed to simplify the process of building and using
polyglot programming environments. While existing solutions have their strengths
at various levels, they do not cover the complete spectrum of integrating these languages (*pidgin, creole and argot languages*); and existing solutions usually do not reuse
conventional tools (*conventional language and tools*).

The EBNF language should coexist with the host and possibly with other languages
(*multiple context-dependent languages*). This co-habitation should be transparent in
the sense that objects can be passed through code written in multiple languages (*homogeneous code and data abstraction*). Furthermore, the environment should provide
development tools — like syntax highlighting and debugging — that can be used
uniformly across different languages (*homogeneous tool support*).

In Section 1.2 we have identified and described these five requirements for embedding and combining multiple languages into a single host environment:

Pidgin, Creole and Argot Languages. A general approach for language embedding
needs to support different kinds of languages. The example of the EBNF is a
creole language.

Multiple Context-Dependent Languages. Different languages and the host language
should be mixable in arbitrary ways. Language changes should not be limited to file boundaries, but depend on the location in the source code only.
In the example of the EBNF language extension we would like to define the
grammar close together with the associated production actions that are specified using the host language syntax.

Homogeneous Tool Support. Language users demand sophisticated tool support for
the languages they are using. For example, they would like to step with a
single debugger through a method that mixes various languages. To debug a
grammar definition, we would like to be able to step both through EBNF and
through the production actions using the debugger of the host environment.

Homogeneous Code and Data Abstraction. It should be possible to pass values from one language to another without requiring a conversion in-between. In our running example we would like to directly access and use the grammar and the resulting AST from within the host language.

Conventional Language and Tools. Most important, a conventional language and development environment should be leveraged as the host instead of introducing a new or derived one. This avoids compatibility problems with existing code and lets developers use their accustomed development tools.

8.2 Requirements for a Host Environment

The most basic approach is to derive a new pseudo-language from an existing API, an *internal DSL*. While this approach fulfills all the above requirements, it is often not powerful enough since the language is constrained by the syntax and the semantics of the host environment. Instead of using the concise EBNF language constructs we would need to express grammars using a verbose series of message sends written in the host language.

Systems with *meta-programming* facilities like Scheme, Converge and MetaOCaml avoid this problem by providing compile-time code generation, however they often lack sophisticated tool support. Similarly, *extensible compilers* like JastAdd or Xoc allow language designers to tweak the host language compiler, but usually do not provide a way to integrate the modified language into the existing tools. None of the systems offers tight IDE integration, and the transformed code cannot be debugged at the source level.

Language workbenches like JetBrain MPS or Intentional Software come with a specialized IDE for language engineering. They provide a special workflow to define new languages and they provide tools for language development and application. The problem with these approaches is that they do not build on top of existing tools and host languages, but provide their own custom host environment instead.

Helvetia follows a different approach: Our idea is to chose an existing host environment and to extend its compiler and programming environment with hook that allow developers to parameterize the tools for language extensions. While such an approach is possible in any general-purpose programming language, there are certain language features that make an implementation more practicable. We have identified the following six features as the most important ones:

1. A *minimal syntax* makes a language a good source and target for program transformation.

2. A language with *dynamic semantics* gives developers more flexibility at the level of libraries, without forcing them to immediately resort to the language implementation.

3. A *reflective language* makes the structure and behavior of a system observable and changeable. This is crucial for tools as well as the language extensions themselves.

4. A *homoiconic language* is a language where the representation of behavior and data is the same [Mooers and Deutsch, 1965]. Consequently it is easy to generate new and change existing behavior.

5. A *homogeneous environment* is an environment where the tools are written in the host language itself. Again this makes them viable for change.

6. Being able to change a language and its tools *on-the-fly* makes the development process faster and quick language experiments feasible.

8.3 Host Language Shootout

	C++	C#	Java	Javascript	Lisp	Ruby	Smalltalk
8.3.1 Minimal Syntax	○	○	○	○	●	○	●
8.3.2 Dynamic Semantics	○	◐	○	●	●	●	●
8.3.3 Reflective Language	◐	◐	◐	◐	●	◐	◐
8.3.4 Homoiconic Language	○	○	○	○	●	○	●
8.3.5 Homogeneous Environment	○	○	◐	◐	◐	○	●
8.3.6 On-the-fly Changes	○	○	○	◐	◐	◐	●

Table 8.1: Comparison of different main-stream programming languages and their suitability for language engineering. Legend: ○ no support, ◐ partial support, ● full support.

In this section we present the case for why Smalltalk has practical benefits over other programming languages. Table 8.1 provides a summary of the features supported by the considered programming languages: a filled circle denotes that the language fully supports the given feature, while a half-filled circle means that the feature is only partially supported or that it requires additional workarounds to access it. Each of the features is presented in detail in the following subsections.

8.3.1 Minimal Syntax

The obvious winner in this area are Lisp-like languages. This family of programming languages provides s-expressions (parenthesized lists) as their central language construct. This means that source code is written in an extremely uniform way that is directly related to the abstract syntax tree. As such Lisp is well suited for macro programming.

As a metric for minimal syntax we count the number of AST nodes used in a typical compiler of the contending languages. Table 8.2 lists these results retrieved from various open-source implementations of the respective languages.

Language	Implementation	AST Nodes
C++	gcc 4.5.0	262
C#	DotGNU 0.1	225
Java	Open JDK 7	111
Ruby	Ruby 1.9.1	109
Javascript	V8 2.3.3	41
Smalltalk	Pharo Smalltalk 1.0	10
Lisp	CLISP 2.49	2

Table 8.2: Number of AST nodes as a measurement of syntactical complexity.

Smalltalk has a minimal syntax[1], and Smalltalk compilers rarely have more than ten different node types to support the full language. Depending on the implementation details, the following node types are supported:

1. A *method node* describes the method signature and method body.

2. A *pragma node* describes method annotations and their arguments.

3. A *sequence node* describes a sequence of statements and a preceding declaration of temporary variables.

4. A *message send node* describes a method invocation on a receiver with a given set of arguments.

5. A *cascade node* describes a series of message sends to the same receiver.

6. A *block node* describes a block closure and its arguments.

7. A *return node* describes a return from a method or block.

8. A *variable node* describes a temporary, instance or global variable reference.

---

1 Jokingly it is often remarked that a description of the syntax would fit on a postcard.

9. An *assignment node* describes a variable assignment.

10. A *literal node* describes literal values, such as numbers, characters, strings, symbols or boolean values.

The rest of the language features stem from the Smalltalk library. Contrary to most other programming languages, control structures are modeled using message sends and block closures, thus the compiler does not require specific node types to handle these.

The simplicity of Smalltalk makes it an attractive target for language transformation both from arbitrary languages to Smalltalk or within the Smalltalk language itself. In the first case a parser can directly build a Smalltalk AST, in simple cases just consisting of a series of message sends. Transformations within the language only need to match a few basic cases to cover the complete language specification.

In the example of the EBNF language we transform the input into a series of message sends that construct an object model of the grammar. The example grammar presented in Section 8.1 is transformed to the AST of the following two Smalltalk methods:

```
digit
    ^ $0 asParser to: $9 asParser
```

```
number
    ^ $- asParser optional , self digit plus , ($. asParser , self digit plus)
    optional
```

8.3.2 Dynamic Semantics

Most popular programming languages provide static built-in types that have fixed semantics and that cannot be changed. Furthermore, it is often not possible to extend the existing system or library classes with new code (*e.g.*, Java). C# provides an extension mechanism through partial classes, however this mechanism does not allow us to extend existing tools as the partial class and its extensions must reside in the same compilation unit. In dynamic languages like Ruby and Javascript it is typically possible to extend existing classes.

Smalltalk is built around objects, polymorphism and dynamic dispatch. This together with the fact that everything happens by message passing is an advantage when it comes to changing the semantics. For example, to change the default lower index of arrays of 1 to something else is a matter of creating a custom subclass of `Array` and overriding the methods `at:` to read and `at:put:` to write an array cell.

In the example of the EBNF language we extended the classes of common Smalltalk literals with the method `asParser`, so that these objects can be converted to a parsers that accept themselves. This is used in the transformed code to construct a parser for a character. `$0 asParser` returns a parser that parses the character '0'.

However, even though it is advertised that everything in Smalltalk happens by message passing, this is not entirely true. For example, reading from and writing to temporary, instance and global variables is not performed using a message send, but through primitive bytecodes. This is a problem when state-access needs to be reified and should be made accessible in a more dynamic way. Other programming languages like Self, Ruby, Javascript and Python are more dynamic in that regard.

Bracha *et al.* [Bracha, 2007] have demonstrated with *NewSpeak* that we can build a Smalltalk-like system that accesses state through message sends only. This presents the advantage that state access can be overridden and intercepted as it is currently done with method polymorphism. Intercepting state changes is useful to automatically notify observers that are interested in how a particular object changes.

8.3.3 Reflective Language

Helvetia heavily depends on the reflective features of the host language. We use the reflective infrastructure to scope language extensions to classes, class hierarchies, packages, *etc.* The EBNF language extension is for example scoped to the subclasses of a generic parser class.

While most mainstream programming languages have good support for introspection, they often lack sophisticated support to perform structural changes at runtime [Tanter, 2009]. Being able to create new classes and to change behavior of existing objects is useful for many embedded languages.

Unfortunately only few mainstream programming languages (*e.g.*, Javascript) provide rich structural and computational reflection. Even fewer provide support that goes beyond basic structural reflection at the level of classes or methods. C# 3.0 provides only partial access to the AST of statically declared expressions using expression trees. Only in few languages like Lisp and Smalltalk we do have direct access to the AST. Although Helvetia does not strictly require reflective facilities to change the running application, having read-write access to the AST greatly simplified its implementation.

Helvetia performs code transformations on the same AST nodes that are also used by the host language compiler. While this is not a requirement, this avoids code duplication in parser, compiler and other tools. Instead of relying on source-to-source transformations, a single uniform code representation is used. This approach allows us to keep accurate source location information, which is crucial to facilitate contextual error reporting and highlighting in the debugger as depicted in Figure 8.1.

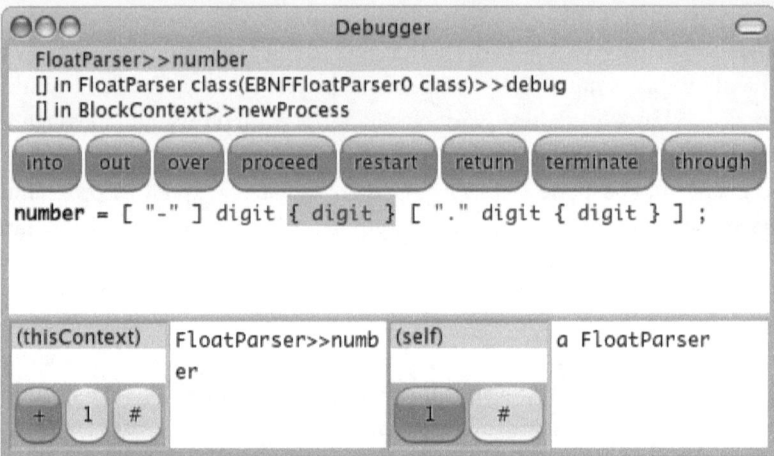

Figure 8.1: Stepping through a mixture of EBNF and the host language using the standard debugger.

Smalltalk and most other main-stream programming lack features that are central to meta-programming. Traditionally code fragments are specified using strings. This leads to fragile code and makes it difficult to debug, as the origin of the code cannot be tracked. A slightly better solution is to manually instantiate and compose the AST nodes. In this case the origin can be tracked, but the code is still hard to read and debug.

The quasiquoting facilities presented in Section 4.1.2 simplify the code transformation from our EBNF example to host language code. The three examples below show different approaches to generate a small part of the code we saw in action in Figure 8.1. Specifically we show how the repeat statement is generated:

1. String Concatenation. The most trivial way to do this is to (1) print out the inner node, (2) concatenate it with the repeat message which is part of the API of the language grammar model and returns a repeat clause, and (3) re-parse the complete string. Code like this is hard to debug and with pretty printing and parsing origin information is lost. Furthermore, repeatedly parsing and pretty printing code is also inefficient.

```
Parser parseExpression: '(' , aNode prettyPrinted , ') repeat'
```

2. Manual AST Composition. Another option consists in manually constructing the AST. In this case the node is composed with the `repeat` message. This approach works reasonably well, but it gets cumbersome in more complicated cases. The compiler cannot check up front if the resulting code is valid and it is not immediately obvious for developers to see what code gets generated.

```
RBMessageNode receiver: aNode selector: #repeat
```

3. Quasiquoting. Using the introduced quasiquoting facilities code is easily generated. Furthermore, it is immediately visible what kind of code is generated and the compiler can validate the code generation in advance.

```
``(`,aNode repeat)
```

The presented quasiquoting language extension to Smalltalk is simple and does not conflict with the existing syntax. The fact that Smalltalk entirely lacks sophisticated facilities for code generation could be fixed by implementing quasiquoting as a language extension.

For a detailed comparison of the reflective features in different programming languages we refer the reader to the work of Bracha *et al.* [Bracha and Ungar, 2004].

8.3.4 Homoiconic Language

None of today's popular programming languages provide out of the box support for the use of different parsers and compilers. Thus people have to use a source-to-source transformation in a pre-compilation phase or rely on a custom compiler. This leads to various problems: (1) the interaction between different languages is difficult, (2) incompatibilities exist between the custom AST representations and the domain models involved, and (3) it is often not possible to trace the transformed code back to the original source.

Homoiconic language were first mentioned in the context of Lisp [Mooers and Deutsch, 1965]. In this language the similarity between code and data is even more visible. *Reader macros* are used to read and transform the source code to s-expressions. Common Lisp comes with a set of reader macros that define the standard language, and custom ones can be added by developers to extend and change the syntax of the host language. The system knows about all the active reader macros and uses s-expressions as the common representation of data and code.

In Smalltalk classes can define a custom parser and compiler by overriding the method `compilerClass`. Helvetia does so by overriding this method in `Object`, the root of the class hierarchy. This enables Helvetia to return a more sophisticated facade object that scopes language changes even further, not only at the level of classes, but also at the level of methods and at the sub-method level. As the parser, the compiler and the executable bytecode are fully accessible using the reflective environment, any part of the system can be customized, extended or even replaced.

Since all executable code eventually ends up in a compiled method object that the VM knows how to interpret, any code can be invoked without knowing its origin. As the object model is the one of the host system, objects can be transparently passed around and used by different language extensions. Thus, different languages can live homogeneously next to each other and interact in a natural and transparent way.

For example, our EBNF language would just return a series of parse tokens by default. To attach production actions to the grammar we need to be able to intermix the EBNF with normal Smalltalk code. In the excerpt below we show that we can use normal Smalltalk code to define a production action right after the grammar specification. In this case `aToken` implicitly refers to the character consumed. We use normal host language code to convert this character into a number:

```
digit = "0" | "1" | ... | "9" ;
   aToken asciiValue - $0 asciiValue
```

Language extensions are scoped to certain parts of the system (*e.g.*, specific classes or packages). When using the reflective facilities of the host system, different languages are aware of each other and can be closely integrated.

8.3.5 Homogeneous Environment

Eclipse, NetBeans and IntelliJ IDEA are full featured Java IDEs implemented in Java. As such, these IDEs provide homogeneous tools that can be extended through an expressive plugin architecture. However, developers are restricted to the provided interface and are often required to restart the complete IDE when a plugin changes.

The Emacs editor provides with Slime an IDE for Lisp development. However, this setup does not provide a homogeneous environment: the tools in Emacs are written in Emacs Lisp and they communicate through RPC with a Swank-Backend that eventually connects to the Lisp compiler. LispWorks is an IDE for Lisp development resembling Smalltalk IDEs. While it provides a rich API to extend its tools, the source code is not available and thus the developer is restricted to the provided extension points.

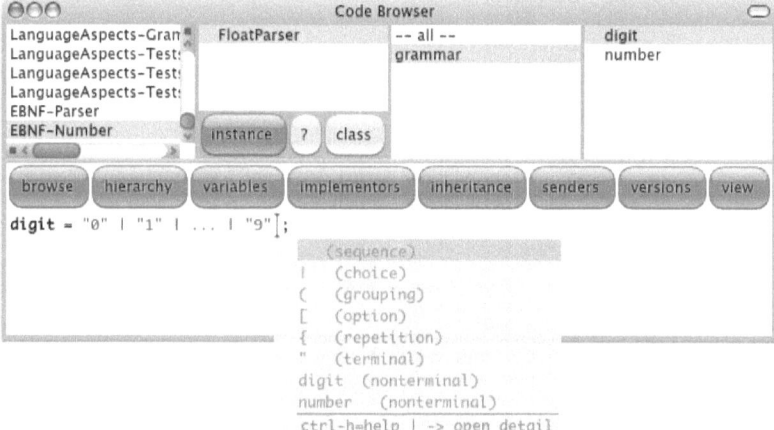

Figure 8.2: The "Code Browser" opened on the EBNF language with adapted syntax highlighting and auto completion.

Arguments similar to those given in the previous section can also be given in relation to tools integration. In Smalltalk all development tools are implemented themselves and can be modified on the fly. This makes it easy for building and integrating languages into these tools. Since the tools rely on the reflection facilities, many parts of the editors can be changed just by providing different answers to their queries. For example:

- *Syntax highlighting* (see Figure 8.2) is typically implemented by traversing the parse-tree of the edited method. As long as this tree can be properly visited by the syntax highlighter, the code editors do not care about the language that is being edited. The only information a language extension needs to provide is some color and style information so that the parse-tree tokens can be highlighted accordingly.

- *Code completion* (see Figure 8.2) typically works on the parse-tree. Language extensions are able to provide possible completion tokens that are presented to the developer.

- *Code debugging* (see Figure 8.1) works at the bytecode level. To highlight the current execution position in the source code, the debugger uses a source map provided by the compiler that encodes text ranges to bytecodes. By providing a custom source map, it is possible to accurately step through a mixture of different languages with a single debugger. The debugger interprets the bytecodes and uses the source map regardless of how the language looks like to the developers.

Having the live source code of all tools at hand is a big advantage for efficient language development and integration. In Smalltalk the compiler, editor, debugger, *etc.* can be changed, adapted or extended without limiting the developer to a plugin architecture imposed by the vendor.

8.3.6 On-the-fly Changes

The image encapsulates the running Smalltalk system. It includes all objects, all classes and their source code, and the currently executed threads. An image can be saved to the file-system at any time and in any state, and re-run on a different machine. When working in a Smalltalk system, code is compiled and installed into the running system. The typical edit-compile-run cycle is avoided and as soon as the source code is edited, it is automatically compiled and used by the running system.

Having an ever running system makes it viable to quickly develop and test new language features in the context of a domain. The language change is immediately available and can be tested in the running system using the objects already present.

When a language definition changes, it is often required that the users of this language are recompiled. In a reflective system like Smalltalk the clients of a language can be enumerated and asked to recompile themselves. This is a similar query to the functionality of displaying senders and implementors of a particular method selector.

While many dynamic languages (*e.g.*, Lisp, Ruby, Javascript) provide similar functionality through their interactive consoles, they do not take it as far as Smalltalk does. For example, it is often not possible to fix a bug from within the debugger, or to change the way the console works while it is running. The fact that source code primarily lives in files, makes it hard to interact with the code using a first-class representation.

However, Smalltalk being an ever living object space presents also practical disadvantages: It makes it difficult to change certain parts of the system, *e.g.*, changing the compiler while it is being used to compile its own source code. To circumvent these types of problems we always keep the original compiler around so that it can replace the default compiler in case something goes wrong.

Another related problem is that language extensions need to be available before any of the client code is loaded. This enforces that language extensions are packaged and loaded separately beforehand.

8.4 Conclusion

Context specific languages are languages that are embedded in a host language, but active only within certain well-defined contexts. Embedding such new languages into an existing host environment is currently not well supported. To accommodate them we need to extend an existing language with a proper environment.

Helvetia expresses foreign languages in terms of the AST of the host language. This is the shortest path to reusing the host language tools, if they all work on the standard reflective facilities of the host language's code model.

The contribution of this chapter is to distill our experience of using Smalltalk as the host language. We considered multiple language environments from the point of view of their suitability as possible hosts. In essence, we argue that Smalltalk is a prime candidate for a system like Helvetia. Other languages considered (as seen in Table 8.1) fall short from various points of view. Lisp is a strong contender, however it lacks support of having full access to compiler and tools in the running system.

While Smalltalk is a good practical solution, it still is not ideal. To easily specify code transformation we had to extend the language with a quasiquoting mechanism. Another problem is that Smalltalk does not give us access to the execution semantics of the VM. Accommodating a language that is not message-based (*e.g.*, Prolog or Haskell) is difficult and requires mapping the semantics of the new language [Wuyts, 2001] to the message-based one of the Smalltalk VM.

Chapter 9

Conclusions

> *"Knowing is not enough, we must apply. Willing is not enough, we must do."*
> — Johann Wolfgang von Goethe

In this last chapter we summarize the contributions made by this dissertation and point to directions for future work.

9.1 Contributions of the Dissertation

We set out to address the shortcomings of existing approaches to language embedding. We argued that an explicit first-class model for language extensions is needed to support context-dependent embedded languages that do not break existing tools.

Our key contributions are the following:

- We have identified (Chapter 1) three fundamental types of embedded languages: *pidgins* adapt the syntax of the host language while extending its semantics; *creoles* further refine pidgins with their own dedicated syntax; and *argots* switch the semantics of the host language without changing the syntax.

- We have presented (Chapter 3) a novel approach to language embedding by leveraging the host language toolchain with a common rule system. This achieves a tight integration of different languages with the host language and the existing tools.

- We have shown (Chapter 5) how a first-class language model enables fine-grained language changes, language composition and language re-use in terms of dynamic grammar transformations (Chapter 6).

- We have identified the key requirements for a host language implementing a system like Helvetia (Chapter 8); and we have validated our implementation against various language and tool extensions (Chapter 4, Chapter 7, Appendix A, and Appendix B).

9.2 Impact of Helvetia

Helvetia has already seen some use in research, both at the University of Bern and other research groups. We briefly survey current and possibly upcoming uses of Helvetia:

- The *Moose analysis platform* [Nierstrasz et al., 2005] employs various internal domain-specific languages to describe their code models, visualizations and browsers. Already today the parsing infrastructure of Helvetia is part of Moose and the authors plan to further improve their domain-specific languages with Helvetia.

- The authors of *Reflectivity* [Denker et al., 2007b] have expressed their interest employing the quasiquoting mechanism of Helvetia to improve the usability of their on-the-fly code generation through AST annotations. To inject behavior into running applications they currently manually manipulate AST nodes or use extra indirections through block closures. The use of Helvetia's quasiquoting mechanisms would avoid the breakage of tools and debuggers.

- The authors of the logic query engine *SOUL* [Wuyts and Ducasse, 2001] have built an initial prototype tightly integrating their logical queries into Smalltalk using Helvetia. The existing approach directly patched various tools and thus made it difficult to mix and match queries with host language code. With the adaption to Helvetia these limitations disappeared.

- Krasemann *et al.* [Krasemann et al., 2010] applied Helvetia for building a DSL for *Harel-Statecharts* in the context of their research on integrated learn and development environments.

- *Pharo Smalltalk* [Black et al., 2009] is a clean, innovative, open-source Smalltalk environment. The Pharo board has expressed its interest to integrate the core Helvetia infrastructure as part of the Pharo distribution to make the language and programming environment easier to extend and open-up new spaces for research and experimentation.

Furthermore, our work on Helvetia has influenced and has been influenced by various open-source and industrial projects:

- The *Refactoring Engine* [Roberts, 1999] provides the cornerstones for code matching in Helvetia. With our work on Helvetia we have revived the refactoring tools and improved their integration into the host environment. *Omni-Browser* [Bergel et al., 2008] is an extensible browser framework aiming to replace the traditional Smalltalk tools. We have significantly improved Omni-Browser with new features that are useful in a context beyond Helvetia. As of today, both the Refactoring Engine and OmniBrowser are part of the standard development tools shipped with Pharo Smalltalk.

- The *New Compiler* [Hannan, 2004] is an alternative compiler for *Pharo Smalltalk* avoiding the monolithic design of the original Smalltalk-80 compiler. Helvetia was initially developed using the New Compiler infrastructure, but has recently reverted to the bytecode generator of the original Smalltalk-80 compiler. The change was necessary to support newer versions of Pharo Smalltalk that employ alternative byte codes for closure creation and activation. Our work with both compilers led to various improvements in these frameworks.

- *Glamour* [Bunge, 2009] is a model to build browsers from components and connectors. We were involved in the development of an internal domain-specific language to specify the layout and flow of data in Glamour browsers. Glamour is widely applied in the context of the Moose platform for software and data analysis to build custom user interfaces to explore large models.

- *Seaside* [Ducasse et al., 2007] is a popular web application framework employing various internal domain-specific languages for HTML generation, Javascript generation, page composition, control flow specification and server configuration. *Magritte* [Renggli et al., 2007] is a self-described meta-modeling framework. It uses an internal domain-specific language to create meta-models and interpret these meta-models to automate the creation of user-interfaces, reports, persistency, and data querying. Both frameworks inspired our work on domain-specific languages and language embedding.

9.3 Future Research Directions

Contextually Customized User Interfaces. Helvetia currently supports only source-code related user-interface changes (code highlighting, code completion, *etc.*). The programming environment itself — browsers for packages, classes and methods; object inspectors; debuggers — does not contextually adapt to different languages. We plan to extend the language box model with specifications on how to adapt the standard tools depending of the context they are used in. A debugger could for example decide to hide the host language stack frames in the context of SQL and instead display some performance statistics from the database backend. We imagine to apply *Glamour* [Bunge, 2009] as a quick mean to script these new user-interfaces.

Support for Language Evolution. Changing the implementation of an embedded language does not automatically recompile code that currently uses this language. While Helvetia can point the developer to such inconsistent code, it does not provide any help in updating this code. We envision to apply the approach of *Change Boxes* [Denker *et al.*, 2007a] to encapsulate language definitions as versioned first-class entities, that support multiple, concurrent and possibly inconsistent language extensions. Furthermore, it would be interesting to provide transformations to automatically update language users as the language evolves.

Language Boxes for Statically Typed Languages. Statically typed languages make a model like Language Boxes more difficult to implement due to the additional constraints not present in our implementation. We currently have a prototypical pre-compiler for Java that can be used to parse a file with a transformed grammar and to pretty print the result to standard Java code. This approach evades the problem of type checking, but it also does not provide the key advantages like tool integration and fine-grained scoping. However, it demonstrates that the Language Box model is viable for statically typed languages with a considerably more complex syntax than Smalltalk. Further research could provide a model that does not show these weaknesses.

Host Language Migration. IDEs need to provide mechanisms to build common types of DLSs automatically. The development environment could suggest where and how the developer should migrate code to use a DSL, and automatically perform this refactoring based on the language definitions.

Appendix A

Getting Started

This appendix gives instructions on how to install, implement and deploy language extensions with the Helvetia system.

A.1 Installation

There are two ways to get the Helvetia system. The recommended quick and easy way is to use the pre-built one-click distribution.

A.1.1 Downloading a One-Click Distribution

1. Download the one-click Helvetia distribution from `http://scg.unibe.ch/research/helvetia`.

2. Launch the executable of your platform:

   - Mac: `Helvetia.app`
   - Linux: `Helvetia.app/Helvetia.sh`
   - Windows: `Helvetia.app/Helvetia.exe`

A.1.2 Building a Custom Image

1. Get a Pharo-Core image from `http://www.pharo-project.org/`.

2. Add the Monticello repository of Helvetia:

```
MCHttpRepository
    location: 'http://source.lukas-renggli.ch/helvetia'
    user: ''
    password: ''
```

3. Load the latest version of the package `Helvetia-Loader`. This will automatically load all the dependencies and patch your system to give Helvetia the necessary entry points.

A.2 A First Language Extension: Roman Numbers

The goal of this simple language extension is to add roman numbers into the host language. This pidgin language keeps the syntax of the host-language and re-interprets variables that are roman numbers as their respective numbers.

We start out by defining a class that tests the language extension and that holds the Helvetia transformation rules:

```
TestCase subclass: #RomanNumberExample
    instanceVariableNames: ''
    classVariableNames: ''
    poolDictionaries: ''
    category: 'Helvetia-Examples'
```

As a first step we define the transformation rule on the class-side of `RomanNumberExample`. This rule is automatically picked up by the compiler for all instance-side code of the class and potential subclasses.

```
 1  RomanNumberExample class>>transformRoman
 2      <transform>
 3
 4      ^ CHTreePattern new
 5          expression: '`var' do: [ :context |
 6              | arabic |
 7              arabic := context node name romanNumber.
 8              arabic notNil
 9                  ifTrue: [ context node replaceWith: arabic lift ] ];
10          yourself
```

The code works as follows:

- Line 2 tells the compiler that the rule should be applied after parsing and before performing the semantic analysis.

- Lines 4–5 instantiate an AST pattern and defines the scope of this rule to all variable nodes in the AST.

- Lines 6–9 define the transformation on the matched variables. Line 7 exacts the variable name from the AST and tries to convert it to a roman number. If the conversion is successful (line 8) the matched variable node is replaced with its arabic value (line 9). The lift converts the integer to a literal node of the host language AST.

To test the code we add a test method to the instance-side:

```
RomanNumberExample>>testAdd
    self assert: III + IV = VII
```

The test should pass when being run. Furthermore, we can verify our transformation by looking at the decompiled code:

```
RomanNumberExample>>testAdd
    "(decompiled code)"
    self assert: 3 + 4 = 7
```

To add syntax highlighting to our language extension we define another Helvetia rule.

```
1   RomanNumberExample class>>highlightRoman
2       <highlight>
3
4       ^ CHTreePattern new
5           expression: '`var' do: Color gray;
6           verification: [ :context | context node romanNumber notNil ];
7           yourself
```

Similarly to the transformation rule we use a tree pattern on all variables. Line 5 defines the color to be used and line 6 gives as an additional precondition that the node is a real roman number.

Editors and debuggers should now present the roman numbers in gray. Stepping through the code with the debugger should work.

A.3 A First Language Box: Regular Expressions

Many programming languages do not have support for literal regular expressions, but instead require the developer to use an external library. The regular expressions have to be created from strings at runtime which is cumbersome and can bring a significant runtime overhead.

```
Regexp fromString: '\w+@\w+\.\w+'
```

In this example we want to extend the host language grammar with support for first-class regular expressions, so that we can use regular expressions like /\w+@\w+\.\w+/ anywhere in host language statements.

To define the language box we create a new subclass of LBLanguageBox called RegularExpressionBox.

```
LBLanguageBox subclass: #RegularExpressionBox
    instanceVariableNames: ''
    classVariableNames: ''
    poolDictionaries: ''
    category: 'Helvetia-Examples'
```

As a first step we define how the grammar of the host language is changed by over-riding the change: method:

```
1  RegularExpressionBox>>change: aGrammar
2      ^ LBChange new
3          before: (aGrammar productionAt: #primary);
4          fragment: ($/ asParser , $/ asParser negate star , $/ asParser) token
```

Line 3 defines where in the original grammar we want to extend the language. Line 4 injects a new grammar fragment into the host language. The (simplified) grammar for this language extension is defined as the slash character '/', followed by several non-slash characters, and ended with the slash character. For the actual parsing of the regular expression itself we reuse existing code as we will see shortly.

At this point we can already test our language box. Create a new test class. Then activate the language box in the context of the class by left clicking onto the class name and selecting *Language Boxes | Add... | RegularExpressionBox*. Then we define the following method that uses our language extension:

```
RegularExpressionBoxTest>>testEmail
    self assert: (/\w+@\w+\.\w+/ matches: 'renggli@gmail.com')
```

When we run the test it fails. This is because we did not specify how the parse-tree should be transformed to the host language AST. By default the language box just inserts a null node that causes the error we observe in the test.

To define the behavior of the language box we specify the compilation concern:

```
RegularExpressionBox>>compile: aToken
    ^ (aToken value copyFrom: 2 to: aToken size - 1) asRegex
        lift: aToken
```

In this example we take the parsed token aToken, remove the slashes from beginning and end, transform it at compile-time to a regular expression object, and lift this object into a literal node. Note that by using lift: aToken we tell the language box the origin of this AST node, so that it can be properly highlighted in the debugger.

From the context menu on RegularExpressionBox select *Language Boxes | Recompile Users* to recompile all the users of the language box. The test should now successfully pass.

To make our language extension appear with a distinct color we can add a highlighting concern:

```
RegularExpressionBox>>highlight: aToken
    ^ aToken -> Color orange
```

The change is immediately visible in all code editors.

While this example is simple and only delegates to an existing regular expression implementation Language Boxes can be used for much more complex language embeddings. Check out the example LAPathBox that implements a XPath like query language, or LASqlBox that embeds SQL into the host language.

Appendix B

Examples

This appendix provides an exhaustive list of language extensions that have been implemented in Helvetia. Each extension is shortly described and a small example is given demonstrating its use in practice. Table B.1 categorizes all the language extensions into pidgin, creole and argot languages; and summarizes the infrastructure used and their implementation size.

B.1 Roman Numbers

A simple language extension that adds roman number literals to the host language. A detailed description of its implementation can be found in Section A.2. This implementation consists of 2 Helvetia rules using 14 lines of code. The same language extension implemented using Language Boxes requires only 8 lines of code.

```
self assert: VII = III + IV.
```

B.2 Grammar Definition

This language is used to specify grammars for PEG parsers using an EBNF like syntax. The possibility to use EBNF productions within the code of the host language raises the conciseness of grammar definitions considerably. This language extension is used in Chapter 8. The implementation consists of 3 Helvetia rules using 28 lines of code.

```
digit = "0" | "1" | ... | "9" ;
number = [ "-" ] digit { digit } [ "." digit { digit } ] ;
```

Section	Language	Pidgin	Creole	Argot	Helvetia Rules	Language Boxes	Lines of Code
B.1	Roman Numbers	●	○	○	●	●	8
B.2	Grammar Definition	○	●	○	●	○	28
B.3	SQL	○	●	○	○	●	33
B.4	Regular Expression	○	●	○	○	●	10
B.5	SPath Expression	○	●	○	○	●	17
B.6	Quasiquoting and Unquoting	○	●	○	○	●	53
B.7	Brainfuck Language	○	●	○	●	○	99
B.8	Positional Arguments	●	○	○	○	●	27
B.9	Automaton	○	●	○	●	○	86
B.10	Tuple Space	●	○	○	●	○	100
B.11	Mondrian	●	●	○	●	○	104
B.12	Transactional Memory	○	○	●	●	○	131
B.13	Object Relationships	○	○	●	●	○	16
B.14	String Interpolation	●	○	○	●	○	36
B.15	Assignments and Swapping	●	○	○	●	○	27
B.16	Schematic Tables	○	●	○	○	●	106
B.17	Functional Pattern Matching	○	●	○	●	○	6930
B.18	Message Pipes	○	●	○	○	●	12
B.19	Asynchronous Messages	●	○	○	●	○	24

Table B.1: Overview on different language extensions; their categorization into pidgin, creole and argot languages; the Helvetia infrastructure used and their implementation size.

B.3 SQL

This language extension allows one to use SQL expressions where an expression in the host language is expected. Furthermore, within the SQL expression host language expressions can be embedded using the @(...) construct. A description of this language can be found Section 5.4. The Language Box implementation consists of 33 lines of code, not counting the definition of the SQL grammar.

```
findEmail: aString
   "Retrieve the e-mail for the given username aString."

   | rows |
   rows := SELECT email FROM users
              WHERE username = @(aString).
   ^ rows first first
```

B.4 Regular Expression

Smalltalk does not provide literal regular expressions; with Helvetia this can be changed. A discussion of the implementation can be found in Section 5.1 and Section A.3. The Language Box implementation consists of 10 lines of code.

```
'Nena - 99 Luftballons' =~ /.*\d+.*/
```

B.5 SPath Expression

SPath is a query language which provides a convenient way to access, filter and collect data from a graph of objects. It has similar aims and scope as XPath[1], a query language that is designed to query XML data. The following example assigns all the members of the host language collection `family` which are older than 12 to the host language variable `people`.

```
people := family:members[age > 12]
```

This Language Box implementation of SPath consists of 17 lines of code.

B.6 Quasiquoting and Unquoting

Smalltalk does not provide quasiquoting facilities something that is commonly used in languages like Scheme and Lisp for meta-programming. This language extension is also described in Section 4.1.2 and further discussed in Section 8.3.3. The following code can be used to inline the calculation of the power function. For example, the expression `` `@(self raise: `x to: -4) `` generates the code `1 / (x * x * x * x)`.

---

1 http://www.w3.org/TR/xpath

```
raise: aNode to: anInteger
  anInteger = 0
    ifTrue: [ ^ ``1 ].
  anInteger < 0
    ifTrue: [ ^ ``(1 / `,(self raise: aNode to: anInteger abs)) ].
  ^ ``(`,(self raise: aNode to: anInteger abs - 1) * `,aNode)
```

There are two implementations of quasiquoting: The first one is independent of Helvetia and used to bootstrap the system. It duplicates and modifies the original Smalltalk parser and patches the code generator. The source code for this implementation is more than 1400 lines long. The second equivalent implementation is using the Language Boxes infrastructure and consists of 53 lines of code only.

B.7 Brainfuck Language

Brainfuck is a minimalistic programming language simulating a Turing machine. Being able to have a debugger at hand makes it considerably easier to understand the code examples:

```
This program multiplies two single-digit numbers and displays the result
    correctly if it too has only one digit

,>,>++++++++[<------<------>>-]
<<[>[>+>+<<-]>>[<<+>>-]<<<-]
>>>++++++[<+++++++++>-]<.>
```

The Brainfuck implementation consists of a Brainfuck machine (47 LOC), a Brainfuck parser (30 LOC), and two Helvetia rules (22 LOC).

B.8 Positional Arguments

While most programming languages use positional arguments, Smalltalk uses keyword arguments that interleave the argument values of a method invocation. This can be a problem when interfacing with external libraries written in C. This language extension adds positional arguments to Smalltalk. The Language Box implementation consists of 27 lines of code.

```
aCanvas glTexCoord2f(1.0, 0.0).
aCanvas glVertex3f(-0.2, 0.2, -100.0).
```

B.9 Automaton

A simple language to define automaton or finite-state machines. The following example defines an automata that accepts input of the form c(a|d)+r:

```
init : c -> more
more : a -> more
       d -> more
       r -> end
end :
```

The implementation uses two Helvetia rules (19 LOC), a grammar for the automaton language (40 LOC) and the automaton machine (27 LOC).

B.10 Tuple Space

A tuple space is a form of a shared memory or blackboard architecture. While Smalltalk always passes arguments by value, this language extension adds the possibility to pass values by reference by sending asReference to the variable. This enables functions like read: to bind values to variables outside their scope. The following example implements the fibonacci numbers using a tuple space:

```
fibonacci: anInteger
    | result |
    (space read: {'fib'. anInteger. result asReference} ifNone: [ nil ]) isNil
        ifFalse: [ ^ result ].
    anInteger < 2 ifTrue: [
        space write: { 'fib'. anInteger. 1 }.
        ^ 1 ].
    space write: {'fib'. anInteger. (self fibonacci: anInteger - 1)
        + (self fibonacci: anInteger - 2)}.
    space read: {'fib'. anInteger. ?result}.
    ^ result
```

The implementation uses one Helvetia rule (12 LOC) and a simple implementation of a tuple space (88 LOC).

B.11 Mondrian

Mondrian is a graph based visualization framework that provides a declarative Smalltalk API for users to specify new visualizations and compose existing ones. This language extension makes it possible to define new shapes using a CSS like syntax.

```
shape {
    cols: #grow, #fill;
    rows: #grow, #fill;
}
label {
    position: 1 , 1;
    text: [ :each | each name ];
    borderColor: #black;
    borderWidth: 1;
}
rectangle {
    position: 1 , 2;
    colspan: 2;
    borderColor: #black;
    borderWidth: 1;
    width: 200;
    height: 100;
}
```

The implementation of this language extension is described in Section 4.2 and Section 4.3. It uses two Helvetia rules (15 LOC) and a customized CSS grammar (89 LOC).

B.12 Transactional Memory

Transactional Memory is an example for changing the execution semantics without changing the syntax of the host language. All state changes in the atomic block below are deferred to the end of the transaction so that conflicts can be detected. The details of this language extension are described in Section 4.4.

```
tree := BTree new.
[ tree at: #a put: 1 ] atomic.
```

The implementation consists of one Helvetia rule (19 LOC) and the infrastructure to track object changes within transactions (112 LOC).

B.13 Object Relationships

A common challenge with complex object models is to implement relationships between objects. With this language extension the implementation of the write accessor next: of a double linked list is simple, the code to update the opposite relationship is generated automatically:

```
Link>>next: aLink
  <opposite: #prev>
  next := aLink
```

The implementation uses a single Helvetia rule and consists of 16 lines of code.

B.14 String Interpolation

String interpolation can be error prone and expensive when interpreted at runtime. The following examples demonstrate two flavors of compile-time optimized printf-like language extension:

```
'<1s> owns <2p> pair<3?s:>' << ('Hans' , 1 , false)
'You Smalltalk has {Smalltalk allClasses size} classes'
```

The implementation uses one Helvetia rule to transform the code (29 LOC) and one to highlight the strings (7 LOC).

B.15 Assignments and Swapping

The following example adds the <==> construct to the language to swap the contents of two variables. Furthermore the <== allows one to assign multiple values in one expression:

```
| a b |
{ a. b } <== { 'hello'. 'world' }        "assigns 'hello' to a, and 'world' to b"
a <==> b.                                   "swaps the values of a and b"
```

The implementation uses two Helvetia rules consisting of 27 lines of code.

B.16 Schematic Tables

Schematic Tables provide a convenient way to handle arbitrarily complex conditionals. The following example defines a function from the booleans a, b, and c to the number x. The table below is read column by column: if a is true, then the result is 1; if a is false and b is true or a is false and c is true, then the result is 2, etc. The implementation uses Language Boxes and consists of 106 lines of code.

```
x := {| a  | = true   | = false | = false | = false |}
     {| b  | --       | = true  | --      | = false |}
     {| c  | --       | --      | = true  | = false |}
     {|    | 1        | 2       | 2       | 3        |}.
```

B.17 Functional Pattern Matching

Most object-oriented programming languages dispatch to functions depending on the receiver type only. In functional languages like Haskell or ML it is common to specify case-based functions on argument patterns. This Helvetia language extension adds pattern matching to Smalltalk. The supported patterns for receiver and function arguments are the following:

- The *do not care pattern* matches anything and is specified using lowercase identifier names.

- The *literal pattern* matches host language literals such as nil, true, false, integers, strings, characters and floats.

- The *type pattern* matches a specific type or subtype. It follows the naming convention of argument names: anInteger matches instances and sub-instances of the class Integer.

- The *list pattern* matches collections. { } matches the empty collection, { x } matches the collection with exactly one element, { x | xs } matches the non-empty collection with the head element x and the tail elements xs. Other patterns can nest into the list pattern.

- The *predicate pattern* uses a block closure as a function to decide whether to accept an argument or not.

For example, the `zip` function that transforms two collections {1. 2. 3} zip: {4. 5} to a list of tuples {1 @ 4. 2 @ 5} is implemented as follows:

```
aCollection>>zip: {}
   ^ {}
```

```
{}>>zip: aCollection
   ^ {}
```

```
{x|xs}>>zip: {y|ys}
   ^ {x @ y} , (xs zip: ys)
```

The implementation consists of a custom dispatching infrastructure, a custom parser for the method declarations, and a customized code browser. The complete implementation consists of 6930 lines of code.

B.18 Message Pipes

The classic Smalltalk syntax does allow to chain unary and binary messages without using parentheses like so:

```
1 negated isZero.
1 + 2 + 3 + 4.
```

However, with keyword messages parentheses are required:

```
(((1 to: 10)
   select: [ :each | each odd ])
   collect: [ :each | each * each ])
   inject: 0 into: [ :sum :each | sum + each ]
```

A pipe or chain operator ':>' as proposed by Vassili Bykov[2] makes the result of the preceding expression the receiver of the following message send. So that the above expression can be rewritten without parentheses:

```
(1 to: 10)
    :> select: [ :each | each odd ]
    :> collect: [ :each | each * each ]
    :> inject: 0 into: [ :sum :each | sum + each ]
```

The implementation uses Language Boxes and consists of 12 lines of code. A previously proposed implementation (40 LOC) directly patched the compiler and broke debugger and syntax highlighting.

B.19 Asynchronous Messages

Croquet Smalltalk[3] provides an implementation of asynchronous messages as a patch into the standard compiler and a small amount of support code. The following code shows a traffic light that changes from red, to orange, and to green before it disappears again:

```
morph := CircleMorph new.
morph color: Color red.
(morph future) openInWorld.
(morph future: 1 second) color: Color orange.
(morph future: 2 seconds) color: Color green.
(morph future: 3 seconds) delete.
```

The code fragment immediately returns as the messages openInWorld, color: and delete are sent asynchronously as defined by the future keyword. An optional argument allows one to schedule the message after a given duration in the future.

The implementation of this pidgin language consists of 24 lines of code and uses two Helvetia rules to implement the functionality. The original implementation in Croquet consists of more than 150 lines of code that are directly intertwined with the standard compiler.

---

2 http://blog.3plus4.org/2007/08/30/message-chains/
3 http://www.opencroquet.org/

Appendix C

Bibliography

[Achermann *et al.*, 2001] Franz Achermann, Markus Lumpe, Jean-Guy Schneider, and Oscar Nierstrasz. Piccola — a small composition language. In Howard Bowman and John Derrick, editors, *Formal Methods for Distributed Processing — A Survey of Object-Oriented Approaches*, pages 403–426. Cambridge University Press, 2001.

[Aldrich *et al.*, 2002] Jonathan Aldrich, Craig Chambers, and David Notkin. Architectural reasoning in ArchJava. In *ECOOP'02: Proceedings of the 16th European Conference on Object-Oriented Programming*, volume 2374 of *LNCS*, pages 334–367, Malaga, Spain, 2002. Springer-Verlag.

[Andreae *et al.*, 2006] Chris Andreae, James Noble, Shane Markstrum, and Todd Millstein. A framework for implementing pluggable type systems. In *OOPSLA '06: Proceedings of the 21st annual ACM SIGPLAN conference on Object-oriented programming systems, languages, and applications*, pages 57–74, New York, NY, USA, 2006. ACM Press.

[Baader and Nipkow, 1998] Franz Baader and Tobias Nipkow. *Term Rewriting and All That*. Cambridge University Press, 1998.

[Backus, 1959] John Warner Backus. The syntax and semantics of the proposed international algebraic language of the Zurich ACM-GAMM conference. In *Proceedings of the International Conference on Information Processing*, pages 125–132, 1959.

[Bawden, 1999] Alan Bawden. Quasiquotation in Lisp. In *Partial Evaluation and Semantic-Based Program Manipulation*, pages 4–12, 1999.

[Becket and Somogyi, 2008] Ralph Becket and Zoltan Somogyi. DCGs + Memoing = Packrat parsing, but is it worth it? In *Practical Aspects of Declarative Languages*, volume LNCS 4902, pages 182–196. Springer, January 2008.

[Bentley, 1986] Jon Louis Bentley. Programming pearls: Little languages. *Communications of the ACM*, 29(8):711–721, August 1986.

[Bergel *et al.*, 2008] Alexandre Bergel, Stéphane Ducasse, Colin Putney, and Roel Wuyts. Creating sophisticated development tools with OmniBrowser. *Journal of Computer Languages, Systems and Structures*, 34(2-3):109–129, 2008.

[Bergin and Gibson, 1996] Thomas J. Bergin and Richard G. Gibson. *History of Programming Languages*. ACM Press / Addison Wesley, 1996.

[Black *et al.*, 2009] Andrew Black, Stéphane Ducasse, Oscar Nierstrasz, Damien Pollet, Damien Cassou, and Marcus Denker. *Pharo by Example*. Square Bracket Associates, 2009.

[Brabranda and Schwartzbach, 2007] Claus Brabranda and Michael I. Schwartzbach. The metafront system: Safe and extensible parsing and transformation. *Science of Computer Programming*, 68(1):2–20, 2007.

[Bracha and Ungar, 2004] Gilad Bracha and David Ungar. Mirrors: design principles for meta-level facilities of object-oriented programming languages. In *Proceedings of the International Conference on Object-Oriented Programming, Systems, Languages, and Applications (OOPSLA'04), ACM SIGPLAN Notices*, pages 331–344, New York, NY, USA, 2004. ACM Press.

[Bracha, 2007] Gilad Bracha. Executable grammars in Newspeak. *Electron. Notes Theor. Comput. Sci.*, 193:3–18, 2007.

[Brant *et al.*, 1998] John Brant, Brian Foote, Ralph Johnson, and Don Roberts. Wrappers to the rescue. In *Proceedings European Conference on Object Oriented Programming (ECOOP'98)*, volume 1445 of *LNCS*, pages 396–417. Springer-Verlag, 1998.

[Bravenboer and Visser, 2004] Martin Bravenboer and Eelco Visser. Concrete syntax for objects. Domain-specific language embedding and assimilation without restrictions. In Douglas C. Schmidt, editor, *Proceedings of the 19th ACM SIGPLAN Conference on Object-Oriented Programing, Systems, Languages, and Applications (OOPSLA 2004)*, pages 365–383, Vancouver, Canada, oct 2004. ACM Press.

[Bravenboer and Visser, 2009] Martin Bravenboer and Eelco Visser. Parse table composition. In *Software Language Engineering*, volume LNCS 5452, pages 74–94. Springer, 2009.

[Bravenboer, 1997] Martin Bravenboer. *Exercises in Free Syntax: Syntax Definition, Parsing, and Assimilation of Language Conglomerates*. PhD thesis, Delft University of Technology, December 1997.

[Bunge, 2009] Philipp Bunge. Scripting browsers with Glamour. Master's thesis, University of Bern, April 2009.

[Calcagno *et al.*, 2003] Cristiano Calcagno, Walid Taha, Liwen Huang, and Xavier Leroy. Implementing multi-stage languages using ASTs, GenSym, and Reflection. In *In Krzysztof Czarnecki, Frank Pfenning, and Yannis Smaragdakis, editors, Generative Programming and Component Engineering (GPCE)*, volume 2830 of *LNCS*, pages 57–76. Springer-Verlag, 2003.

[Charles *et al.*, 2009] Philippe Charles, Robert M. Fuhrer, Stanley M. Sutton Jr., Evelyn Duesterwald, and Jurgen J. Vinju. Accelerating the creation of customized, language-specific IDEs in Eclipse. In Shail Arora and Gary T. Leavens, editors, *OOPSLA*, pages 191–206. ACM, 2009.

[Clark *et al.*, 2004] Tony Clark, Andy Evans, Paul Sammut, and James Willans. Applied metamodelling: A foundation for language driven development, 2004.

[Clark *et al.*, 2008] Tony Clark, Paul Sammut, and James Willans. *Superlanguages, Developing Languages and Applications with XMF*, volume First Edition. Ceteva, 2008.

[Cleenewerck, 2003] Thomas Cleenewerck. Component-based DSL development. In *Proceedings of the 2nd international conference on Generative programming and component engineering*, pages 245–264. Springer-Verlag New York, Inc. New York, NY, USA, 2003.

[Cordy, 2006] James R. Cordy. The TXL source transformation language. *Sci. Comput. Program.*, 61(3):190–210, 2006.

[Cox *et al.*, 2008] Russ Cox, Tom Bergan, Austin T. Clements, Frans Kaashoek, and Eddie Kohler. Xoc, an extension-oriented compiler for systems programming. *SIGARCH Comput. Archit. News*, 36(1):244–254, 2008.

[Denker *et al.*, 2007a] Marcus Denker, Tudor Gîrba, Adrian Lienhard, Oscar Nierstrasz, Lukas Renggli, and Pascal Zumkehr. Encapsulating and exploiting change with Changeboxes. In *ICDL'07: Proceedings of the 15th International Conference on Dynamic Languages*, pages 25–49, Lugano, Switzerland, August 2007. ACM Digital Library.

[Denker *et al.*, 2007b] Marcus Denker, Orla Greevy, and Oscar Nierstrasz. Supporting feature analysis with runtime annotations. In *Proceedings of the 3rd International Workshop on Program Comprehension through Dynamic Analysis (PCODA 2007)*, pages 29–33. Technische Universiteit Delft, 2007.

[Deursen and Klint, 1997] Arie van Deursen and Paul Klint. Little languages: Little maintenance?   In S. Kamin, editor, *First ACM-SIGPLAN Workshop on Domain-Specific Languages; DSL'97*, pages 109–127, January 1997.

[Dimitriev, 2004] Sergey Dimitriev. Language oriented programming: The next programming paradigm. *onBoard Online Magazine*, 1(1), November 2004.

[Ducasse *et al.*, 2007] Stéphane Ducasse, Adrian Lienhard, and Lukas Renggli. Seaside: A flexible environment for building dynamic web applications. *IEEE Software*, 24(5):56–63, 2007.

[Earley, 1970] Jay Earley. An efficient context-free parsing algorithm. *Commun. ACM*, 13(2):94–102, 1970.

[Ekman and Hedin, 2007] Torbjörn Ekman and Görel Hedin. The JastAdd extensible Java compiler. In Richard P. Gabriel, David F. Bacon, Cristina Videira Lopes, and Guy L. Steele Jr., editors, *OOPSLA'07: Proceedings of the 22nd Conference on Object-Oriented Programming, Systems, Languages, and Applications*, pages 1–18, Montreal, Quebec, Canada, 2007. ACM Press.

[Faith *et al.*, 1997] Rickard E. Faith, Lars S. Nyland, and Jan F. Prins. KHEPERA: a system for rapid implementation of domain specific languages. In *DSL'97: Proceedings of the Conference on Domain-Specific Languages on Conference on Domain-Specific Languages (DSL), 1997*, pages 19–19, Berkeley, CA, USA, 1997. USENIX Association.

[Foote and Johnson, 1989] Brian Foote and Ralph E. Johnson. Reflective facilities in Smalltalk-80. In *Proceedings OOPSLA '89, ACM SIGPLAN Notices*, volume 24, pages 327–336, October 1989.

[Ford, 2002] Bryan Ford. Packrat parsing: simple, powerful, lazy, linear time, functional pearl. In *ICFP 02: Proceedings of the seventh ACM SIGPLAN international conference on Functional programming*, volume 37/9, pages 36–47, New York, NY, USA, 2002. ACM.

[Ford, 2004] Bryan Ford. Parsing expression grammars: a recognition-based syntactic foundation. In *POPL '04: Proceedings of the 31st ACM SIGPLAN-SIGACT symposium on Principles of programming languages*, pages 111–122, New York, NY, USA, 2004. ACM.

[Fowler, 1999] Martin Fowler. *Refactoring: improving the design of existing code*. Addison-Wesley Professional, 1999.

[Fowler, 2005a] Martin Fowler. Fluent interface, 2005.

[Fowler, 2005b] Martin Fowler. Language workbenches: The killer-app for domain-specific languages, June 2005.

[Fowler, 2010] Martin Fowler. *Domain-Specific Languages*. Addison-Wesley Professional, September 2010.

[Freeman and Pryce, 2006] Steve Freeman and Nat Pryce. Evolving an embedded domain-specific language in Java. In *OOPSLA'06: Companion to the 21st Symposium on Object-Oriented Programming Systems, Languages, and Applications*, pages 855–865, Portland, OR, USA, 2006. ACM.

[Futamura, 1999] Yoshihiko Futamura. Partial evaluation of computation process: An approach to a compiler-compiler. *Higher Order Symbol. Comput.*, 12(4):381–391, 1999.

[Gerrits and Gabriëls, 2005] Dirk Gerrits and René Gabriëls. A comparison of macro systems for extending programming languages. Technical report, March 2005.

[Goldberg and Robson, 1983] Adele Goldberg and David Robson. *Smalltalk 80: the Language and its Implementation*. Addison Wesley, Reading, Mass., May 1983.

[Goldberg and Robson, 1989] Adele Goldberg and Dave Robson. *Smalltalk-80: The Language*. Addison Wesley, 1989.

[Greenfield and Short, 2003] Jack Greenfield and Keith Short. Software factories: assembling applications with patterns, models, frameworks and tools. In *OOPSLA '03: Companion of the 18th annual ACM SIGPLAN conference on Object-oriented programming, systems, languages, and applications*, pages 16–27, New York, NY, USA, 2003. ACM.

[Grimm, 2006] Robert Grimm. Better extensibility through modular syntax. In *PLDI 2006*, pages 38–51. ACM, 2006.

[Grossman, 2007] Dan Grossman. The transactional memory / garbage collection analogy. *SIGPLAN Notices*, 42(10):695–706, 2007.

[Group, 2004] Object Management Group. Meta object facility (MOF) 2.0 core final adopted specification. Technical report, Object Management Group, 2004.

[Hannan, 2004] Anthony Hannan. Squeak Closure Compiler, July 2004. http://wiki.squeak.org/squeak/ClosureCompiler.

[Havelund and Pressburger, 2000] Klaus Havelund and Thomas Pressburger. Model checking Java programs using Java PathFinder. *International Journal on Software Tools for Technology Transfer (STTT)*, 2(4):366–381, 2000.

[Heering et al., 1989] Jan Heering, Paul Klint, and Jan Rekers. Incremental generation of parsers. In *PLDI 1989*, pages 179–191. ACM, 1989.

[Herlihy and Moss, 1993] Maurice P. Herlihy and J. Eliot B. Moss. Transactional memory: Architectural support for lock-free data structures. In *Proceedings of the 20. Annual International Symposium on Computer Architecture*, pages 289–300, 1993.

[Herlihy, 1991]   Maurice P. Herlihy. Wait-free synchronization. *ACM Transactions on Programming Languages and Systems*, 13(1):124–149, January 1991.

[Hoare, 1973]   C. A. R. Hoare. Hints on programming language design. Technical Report CS-TR-73-403, Stanford University, 1973.

[Hovemeyer and Pugh, 2004]   David Hovemeyer and William Pugh. Finding bugs is easy. *ACM SIGPLAN Notices*, 39(12):92–106, 2004.

[Hudak, 1996]   Paul Hudak. Building domain specific embedded languages. *ACM Computing Surveys*, 28(4es), December 1996.

[Hudak, 1998]   Paul Hudak. Modular domain specific languages and tools. In P. Devanbu and J. Poulin, editors, *Proceedings: Fifth International Conference on Software Reuse*, pages 134–142. IEEE Computer Society Press, 1998.

[Hunt and Thomas, 2003]   Andy Hunt and Dave Thomas. *Pragmatic Unit Testing in Java with JUnit*. ThePragmaticProgrammers, 2003.

[Hutton and Meijer, 1996]   Graham Hutton and Erik Meijer. Monadic parser combinators. Technical Report NOTTCS-TR-96-4, Department of Computer Science, University of Nottingham, 1996.

[Hutton, 1992]   Graham Hutton. Higher-order functions for parsing. *Journal of Functional Programming*, 2(3):323–343, 1992.

[Jewell and Abate, 2005]   Elizabeth J. Jewell and Frank R. Abate, editors. *The New Oxford American Dictionary*. Oxford University Press, May 2005.

[Johnson, 1978]   S.C. Johnson. Lint, a C program checker. In *UNIX programmer's manual*, pages 78–1273. AT&T Bell Laboratories, 1978.

[Jones *et al.*, 1993]   Neil J. Jones, Carsten K. Gomard, and Peter Sestoft. *Partial Evaluation and Automatic Program Generation*. Prentice-Hall, 1993.

[Kats *et al.*, 2008]   Lennart C. L. Kats, Martin Bravenboer, and Eelco Visser. Mixing source and bytecode. A case for compilation by normalization. In Gregor Kiczales, editor, *Proceedings of the 23rd ACM SIGPLAN Conference on Object-Oriented Programing, Systems, Languages, and Applications (OOPSLA 2008)*, pages 91–108, Nashville, Tenessee, USA, October 2008. ACM.

[Kilpeläinen and Mannila, 1992]   Pekka Kilpeläinen and Heikki Mannila. Grammatical tree matching. In *Combinatorial Pattern Matching*, pages 162–174. Springer, 1992.

[Klint, 1993]   Paul Klint. A meta-environment for generating programming environments. *ACM Transactions on Software Engineering and Methodology (TOSEM)*, 2(2):176–201, 1993.

[Kohlbecker *et al.*, 1986] Eugene E. Kohlbecker, Daniel P. Friedman, Matthias Felleisen, and Bruce Duba. Hygienic macro expansion. *Symposium on LISP and Functional Programming*, pages 151–161, August 1986.

[Koschke and Simon, 2003] Rainer Koschke and Daniel Simon. Hierarchical reflexion models. In *Proceedings of the 10th Working Conference on Reverse Engineering (WCRE 2003)*, page 36. IEEE Computer Society, 2003.

[Krahn *et al.*, 2007] Holger Krahn, Bernhard Rumpe, and Steven Völkel. Integrated definition of abstract and concrete syntax for textual languages. In *Proceedings of MoDELS 2007*, volume 4735 of *LNCS*, pages 286–300. Springer Verlag, 2007.

[Krahn *et al.*, 2008] Holger Krahn, Bernhard Rumpe, and Steven Völkel. Monti-Core: Modular development of textual domain specific languages. In Richard Paige and Bertrand Meyer, editors, *Proceedings of the 46th International Conference Objects, Models, Components, Patterns (TOOLS-Europe)*, pages 297–315. Springer-Verlag, 2008.

[Krasemann *et al.*, 2010] Hartmut Krasemann, Johannes Brauer, and Christoph Crasemann. Eine DSL für Harel-Statecharts mit PetitParser. Arbeitspapier, NOR-DAKADEMIE Hochschule der Wirtschaft, August 2010.

[Kuhn and Verwaest, 2008] Adrian Kuhn and Toon Verwaest. FAME, a polyglot library for metamodeling at runtime. In *Workshop on Models at Runtime*, pages 57–66, 2008.

[Kuhn *et al.*, 2008] Adrian Kuhn, Bart Van Rompaey, Lea Hänsenberger, Oscar Nierstrasz, Serge Demeyer, Markus Gaelli, and Koenraad Van Leemput. JExample: Exploiting dependencies between tests to improve defect localization. In P. Abrahamsson, editor, *Extreme Programming and Agile Processes in Software Engineering, 9th International Conference, XP 2008*, Lecture Notes in Computer Science, pages 73–82. Springer, 2008.

[Lämmel and Zaytsev, 2010] Ralf Lämmel and Vadim Zaytsev. Recovering grammar relationships for the Java language specification. *Software Quality Journal*, SCAM Special Issue, 2010. To appear.

[Lämmel, 2001] Ralf Lämmel. Grammar adaptation. *FME 2001: Formal Methods for Increasing Software Productivity*, pages 550–570, 2001.

[Leijen and Meijer, 2001] D. Leijen and E. Meijer. Parsec: Direct style monadic parser combinators for the real world, 2001.

[Lieberherr, 1989] Karl J. Lieberherr. Formulations and benefits of the Law of Demeter. *ACM SIGPLAN Notices*, 24(3):67–78, 1989.

[Martin, 1985] James Martin. Fourth generation languages, volume i, principles. *New Jersey*, 1985.

[Meijer and Drayton, 2004] Erik Meijer and Peter Drayton. Static typing where possible, dynamic typing when needed: The end of the cold war between programming languages. In *Proceedings OOPSLA Workshop On The Revival Of Dynamic Languages*, 2004.

[Meijer et al., 2006] Erik Meijer, Brian Beckman, and Gavin Bierman. LINQ: reconciling object, relations and XML in the .NET framework. In *SIGMOD '06: Proceedings of the 2006 ACM SIGMOD international conference on Management of data*, pages 706–706, New York, NY, USA, 2006. ACM.

[Mens et al., 2006] Kim Mens, Andy Kellens, Frédéric Pluquet, and Roel Wuyts. Co-evolving code and design with intensional views — a case study. *Journal of Computer Languages, Systems and Structures*, 32(2):140–156, 2006.

[Mernik et al., 2005] Marjan Mernik, Jan Heering, and Anthony M. Sloane. When and how to develop domain-specific languages. *ACM Comput. Surv.*, 37(4):316–344, 2005.

[Meyer et al., 2006] Michael Meyer, Tudor Gîrba, and Mircea Lungu. Mondrian: An agile visualization framework. In *ACM Symposium on Software Visualization (SoftVis'06)*, pages 135–144, New York, NY, USA, 2006. ACM Press.

[Mooers and Deutsch, 1965] Calvin Mooers and Peter Deutsch. TRAC, a text handling language. In *Proceedings of the 1965 20th national conference*, pages 229–246, New York, NY, USA, 1965. ACM.

[Moors et al., 2008] Adriaan Moors, Frank Piessens, and Martin Odersky. Parser combinators in Scala. Technical report, Department of Computer Science, K.U. Leuven, February 2008.

[Muller et al., 2005a] Pierre-Alain Muller, Franck Fleurey, and Jean-Marc Jézéquel. Weaving executability into object-oriented meta-languages. In S. Kent L. Briand, editor, *Proceedings of MODELS/UML'2005*, volume 3713 of *LNCS*, pages 264–278, Montego Bay, Jamaica, October 2005. Springer.

[Muller et al., 2005b] Pierre-Alain Muller, Philippe Studer, Frédérick Fondement, and Jean Bézivin. Independent web application modeling and development with netsilon. *Software and System Modeling*, 4(4):424–442, November 2005.

[Murphy et al., 1995] Gail Murphy, David Notkin, and Kevin Sullivan. Software reflexion models: Bridging the gap between source and high-level models. In *Proceedings of SIGSOFT '95, Third ACM SIGSOFT Symposium on the Foundations of Software Engineering*, pages 18–28. ACM Press, 1995.

[Nierstrasz *et al.*, 2005] Oscar Nierstrasz, Stéphane Ducasse, and Tudor Gîrba. The story of Moose: an agile reengineering environment. In *Proceedings of the European Software Engineering Conference (ESEC/FSE'05)*, pages 1–10, New York, NY, USA, September 2005. ACM Press. Invited paper.

[Nierstrasz *et al.*, 2009] Oscar Nierstrasz, Marcus Denker, and Lukas Renggli. Model-centric, context-aware software adaptation. In Betty H.C. Cheng, Rogerio de Lemos, Holger Giese, Paola Inverardi, and Jeff Magee, editors, *Software Engineering for Self-Adaptive Systems*, volume 5525 of *LNCS*, pages 128–145. Springer-Verlag, 2009.

[Nystrom *et al.*, 2003] Nathaniel Nystrom, Michael R. Clarkson, and Andrew C. Myers. Polyglot: An extensible compiler framework for Java. In *Compiler Construction*, volume 2622 of *Lecture Notes in Computer Science*, pages 138–152. Springer-Verlag, 2003.

[Odersky, 2007] Martin Odersky. Scala language secification v. 2.4. Technical report, École Polytechnique Fédérale de Lausanne, 1015 Lausanne, Switzerland, March 2007.

[Ousterhout, 1998] John K. Ousterhout. Scripting: Higher level programming for the 21st century. *IEEE Computer*, 31(3):23–30, March 1998.

[Parr, 2007] Terence Parr. *The Definitive ANTLR Reference: Building Domain-Specific Languages*. Pragmatic Programmers, May 2007.

[Piumarta and Warth, 2006] Ian Piumarta and Alessandro Warth. Open reusable object models. Technical report, Viewpoints Research Institute, 2006. VPRI Research Note RN-2006-003-a.

[Pluquet *et al.*, 2009] Frédéric Pluquet, Antoine Marot, and Roel Wuyts. Fast type reconstruction for dynamically typed programming languages. In *DLS '09: Proceedings of the 5th symposium on Dynamic languages*, pages 69–78, New York, NY, USA, 2009. ACM.

[Renggli and Gîrba, 2009] Lukas Renggli and Tudor Gîrba. Why Smalltalk wins the host languages shootout. In *Proceedings of International Workshop on Smalltalk Technologies (IWST 2009)*, pages 107–113, New York, NY, USA, 2009. ACM.

[Renggli and Nierstrasz, 2007] Lukas Renggli and Oscar Nierstrasz. Transactional memory for Smalltalk. In *Proceedings of the 2007 International Conference on Dynamic Languages (ICDL 2007)*, pages 207–221. ACM Digital Library, 2007.

[Renggli and Nierstrasz, 2009] Lukas Renggli and Oscar Nierstrasz. Transactional memory in a dynamic language. *Journal of Computer Languages, Systems and Structures*, 35(1):21–30, April 2009.

[Renggli *et al.*, 2007] Lukas Renggli, Stéphane Ducasse, and Adrian Kuhn. Magritte — a meta-driven approach to empower developers and end users. In Gregor Engels, Bill Opdyke, Douglas C. Schmidt, and Frank Weil, editors, *Model Driven Engineering Languages and Systems*, volume 4735 of *LNCS*, pages 106–120. Springer, September 2007.

[Renggli *et al.*, 2009] Lukas Renggli, Marcus Denker, and Oscar Nierstrasz. Language Boxes: Bending the host language with modular language changes. In *Software Language Engineering: Second International Conference, SLE 2009, Denver, Colorado, October 5-6, 2009*, volume 5969 of *LNCS*, pages 274–293. Springer, 2009.

[Renggli *et al.*, 2010a] Lukas Renggli, Stéphane Ducasse, Tudor Gîrba, and Oscar Nierstrasz. Domain-specific program checking. In Jan Vitek, editor, *Proceedings of the 48th International Conference on Objects, Models, Components and Patterns (TOOLS'10)*, volume 6141 of *LNCS*, pages 213–232. Springer-Verlag, 2010.

[Renggli *et al.*, 2010b] Lukas Renggli, Stéphane Ducasse, Tudor Gîrba, and Oscar Nierstrasz. Practical dynamic grammars for dynamic languages. In *4th Workshop on Dynamic Languages and Applications (DYLA 2010)*, Malaga, Spain, June 2010.

[Renggli *et al.*, 2010c] Lukas Renggli, Tudor Gîrba, and Oscar Nierstrasz. Embedding languages without breaking tools. In Theo D'Hondt, editor, *ECOOP'10: Proceedings of the 24th European Conference on Object-Oriented Programming*, volume 6183 of *LNCS*, pages 380–404, Maribor, Slovenia, 2010. Springer-Verlag.

[Repenning and Ioannidou, 2009] Alexander Repenning and Andri Ioannidou. X-expressions in XMLisp: S-expressions and extensible markup language unite. In *ILC '07: Proceedings of the 2007 International Lisp Conference*, pages 1–11, New York, NY, USA, 2009. ACM.

[Roberts *et al.*, 1997] Don Roberts, John Brant, and Ralph E. Johnson. A refactoring tool for Smalltalk. *Theory and Practice of Object Systems (TAPOS)*, 3(4):253–263, 1997.

[Roberts, 1999] Donald Bradley Roberts. *Practical Analysis for Refactoring*. PhD thesis, University of Illinois, 1999.

[Rutar *et al.*, 2004] Nick Rutar, Christian B. Almazan, and Jeffrey S. Foster. A comparison of bug finding tools for Java. In *Software Reliability Engineering, 2004. ISSRE 2004. 15th International Symposium on*, pages 245–256, 2004.

[Sammet, 1969] Jean Sammet. *Programming Languages: History and Fundamentals*. Prentice Hall, 1969.

[Schwerdfeger and Wyk, 2010] August Schwerdfeger and Eric Van Wyk. Verifiable parse table composition for deterministic parsing. In *Software Language Engineering*, volume LNCS 5969, pages 184–203. Springer, 2010.

[Seaton, 2007] Chris Seaton. A programming language where the syntax and semantics are mutable at runtime. Technical Report CSTR-07-005, University of Bristol, June 2007.

[Seela *et al.*, 2008] Ramesh Seela, Ryan Miller, Derek Chang, Ali Shojaeddini, and Ankit Sengar. FxCop tool evaluation. Technical report, Carnegie Mellon University, March 2008.

[Shaw and Garlan, 1996] Mary Shaw and David Garlan. *Software Architecture: Perspectives on an Emerging Discipline*. Prentice-Hall, 1996.

[Sheard, 2001] Tim Sheard. Accomplishments and research challenges in meta-programming. In *SAIG 2001: Proceedings of the Second International Workshop on Semantics, Applications, and Implementation of Program Generation*, pages 2–44, London, UK, 2001. Springer-Verlag.

[Simonyi *et al.*, 2006] Charles Simonyi, Magnus Christerson, and Shane Clifford. Intentional software. In *OOPSLA '06: Proceedings of the 21st annual ACM SIGPLAN conference on Object-oriented programming systems, languages, and applications*, pages 451–464. ACM, 2006.

[Solmi, 2005] Riccardo Solmi. *Whole Platform*. PhD thesis, University of Bologna, March 2005.

[Spinellis, 2001] Diomidis Spinellis. Notable design patterns for domain specific languages. *Journal of Systems and Software*, 56(1):91–99, February 2001.

[Taha, 2003] Walid Taha. A gentle introduction to multi-stage programming. In *Domain-Specific Program Generation*, pages 30–50, 2003.

[Tanter, 2009] Éric Tanter. Reflection and open implementations. Technical Report TR/DCC-2009-13, University of Chile, November 2009.

[Tolvanen *et al.*, 2007] Juha-Pekka Tolvanen, Risto Pohjonen, and Steven Kelly. Advanced tooling for domain-specific modeling: MetaEdit+. In *Proceedings of the 7th OOPSLA Workshop on Domain-Specific Modeling*, 2007.

[Tratt, 2005] Laurence Tratt. The Converge programming language. Technical Report TR-05-01, Department of Computer Science, King's College London, February 2005.

[Tratt, 2008] Laurence Tratt. Domain specific language implementation via compile-time meta-programming. *ACM TOPLAS*, 30(6):1–40, 2008.

[Van Wyk *et al.*, 2002] Eric Van Wyk, Oege de Moor, Kevin Backhouse, and Paul Kwiatkowski. Forwarding in Attribute Grammars for Modular Language Design. *Lecture Notes in Computer Science*, pages 128–142, 2002.

[Van Wyk *et al.*, 2007] Eric Van Wyk, Lijesh Krishnan, Derek Bodin, and August Schwerdfeger. Attribute grammar-based language extensions for java. In *ECOOP'07: Proceedings of the 21st European Conference on Object-Oriented Programming*, pages 575–599, Berlin, Germany, July 2007. Springer.

[Visser, 1997] Eelco Visser. Scannerless generalized-LR parsing. Technical Report P9707, Programming Research Group, University of Amsterdam, July 1997.

[Visser, 2004] Eelco Visser. Program transformation with Stratego/XT: Rules, strategies, tools, and systems in StrategoXT-0.9. In C. Lengauer et al., editors, *Domain-Specific Program Generation*, volume 3016 of *Lecture Notes in Computer Science*, pages 216–238. Spinger-Verlag, June 2004.

[Walton, 1996] Lisa Walton. Domain-specific languages, 1996.

[Warth and Piumarta, 2007] Alessandro Warth and Ian Piumarta. OMeta: an object-oriented language for pattern matching. In *DLS '07: Proceedings of the 2007 symposium on Dynamic languages*, pages 11–19, New York, NY, USA, 2007. ACM.

[Warth *et al.*, 2008] Alessandro Warth, James R. Douglass, and Todd Millstein. Packrat parsers can support left recursion. In *PEPM '08: Proceedings of the 2008 ACM SIGPLAN symposium on Partial evaluation and semantics-based program manipulation*, pages 103–110, New York, NY, USA, 2008. ACM.

[Watt, 1991] David A. Watt. *Programming Language Syntax and Semantics*. Prentice-Hall, 1991.

[Wexelblat, 1981] Richard Wexelblat. *History of programming languages*. Academic Press, 1981.

[Wirth, 1977] Niklaus Wirth. What can we do about the unnecessary diversity of notation for syntactic definitions? *Commun. ACM*, 20(11):822–823, 1977.

[Wuyts and Ducasse, 2001] Roel Wuyts and Stéphane Ducasse. Symbiotic reflection between an object-oriented and a logic programming language. In *ECOOP 2001 International Workshop on MultiParadigm Programming with Object-Oriented Languages*, 2001.

[Wuyts, 2001] Roel Wuyts. *A Logic Meta-Programming Approach to Support the Co-Evolution of Object-Oriented Design and Implementation*. PhD thesis, Vrije Universiteit Brussel, 2001.

www.ingramcontent.com/pod-product-compliance
Lightning Source LLC
Chambersburg PA
CBHW032016170526
45157CB00002B/724